BURDEN OF A SECRET

A Story of Truth and Mercy in the Face of AIDS

Jimmy Allen

Moorings
Nashville, Tennessee
A Division of The Ballantine Publishing Group, Random House, Inc.

BURDEN OF A SECRET
A Story of Truth and Mercy in the Face of AIDS

Library of Congress Cataloging-in-Publication Data

Allen, Jimmy Raymond, 1927–
Burden of a secret : a story of truth and mercy in
the face of AIDS / Jimmy Allen. — 1st ed.
p.   cm.
Includes bibliographical references.
ISBN 0-345-40091-7 (hardcover)
1. Allen, Jimmy Raymond, 1927—Family.
2. Allen family.   3. AIDS (Disease)—Religious
aspects—Christianity.   4. AIDS (Disease)—Patients
—Family relationships.   5. Baptists—United States
—Biography.   6. Southern Baptist Convention—
Biography.   7. Suffering—Religious aspects—
Christianity.   I. Title.
BX6493.A394   1995
261.8′321969792′0922—dc20
[B]   95-31342
                                                 CIP

Manufactured in the United States of America

2   4   6   8   9   7   5   3   1

First Edition: September 1995

ACKNOWLEDGMENTS

I was told that this book about our lives would write itself. It is not so. The process takes all kinds of people and help. I want to thank those dozens who have come alongside our lives to give counsel, comfort, and confrontation. I specifically want to thank Jarrell McCracken, who wouldn't let me forget my responsibility to tell the story; Barbara Jenkins, who believed in the project from her first hearing of it; Jan Jarboe, who provided great help in the focusing process; Bruce Barbour, who saw it as an important book from his reading of an early draft; my sons, who encouraged me to write it as I see it; Wanda, who walks with me through its pages; and Matt, whose actions speak louder than my words. I want to thank Ken Abraham, whose skill in putting windows and descriptions into ideas and events made the book come to life. I want to thank the people of Big Canoe Chapel who have made the mountains our sanctuary and base of ministry while providing a network of concern and support and encouragement.

I want to dedicate this book with my love and appreciation to Big Canoe Chapel, a people and a place God is blessing in unique ways.

CONTENTS

PART ONE

ONE

SECRET BEGINNINGS

THE TELEPHONE RANG as I opened the door to my Nashville hotel room. It was Thursday, around eleven o'clock, on a dismal, dreary, rain-drenched night in late September 1985. I was fatigued and frustrated. I had spent the day at the office of the Executive Committee of the Southern Baptist Convention, hoping to impart a vision to its Finance Committee of reaching millions of homes with a new cable television network. I had been unsuccessful in my efforts to secure our denominational leaders' increased financial backing for the television ministry.

Physically exhausted, mentally and emotionally drained, I plopped into a chair near the ringing telephone and picked up the receiver. I expected to hear the voice of one of my colleagues explaining his or her negative reactions to my proposals, or possibly offering new angles for negotiation with the keepers of our denomination's national purse strings. Instead, I heard the somber, subdued voice of my son Scott calling from Colorado Springs. He spoke so softly I could barely hear him.

"Dad, a blood bank called a few days ago to tell us that the blood Lydia received when Matthew was born was contaminated with a virus."

"Virus? What kind of virus? What does that mean?"

"AIDS."

"*AIDS!*"

Awful images flooded my mind: *AIDS . . . the news headlines had just told of two children in Florida . . . hemophiliacs . . . AIDS . . . angry and scared crowds burning down their house . . . a kid named White . . . what was his name? . . . Ryan White . . . in a lawsuit in the Midwest . . . concerned and frightened people trying to keep him out of the classroom.*

"Lydia tested positive. Bryan and Matthew tested positive, too. I tested negative."

"And that means?"

"I don't have it. But all three of them do."

All three of them! The thought was staggering . . . unbelievable. My daughter-in-law and our two precious grandchildren had AIDS.

I recently had visited them in Colorado, so their images were vivid in my mind: Lydia—intelligent, perky, undaunted by any challenge; Matt—vibrant, nearly three years old, a survivor of several serious medical operations; and newborn Bryan, who had spent most of his first five months of life inside hospital rooms. Now, suddenly, a surreal death sentence had been pronounced upon their young lives.

My thoughts turned back to my son Scott. "Do you want me to come?" I asked.

"No, not yet. Lydia and I talked it over. I am going to see the pastor tomorrow to tell him about it. We feel that is the responsible thing to do. There are children who have been with our children in Sunday school or in the nursery whose parents will want to get them tested. I'll let you know how things work out."

"Yes," I agreed, feeling numb. "That is the responsible thing to do. Well, I'm available to you. I'll cancel everything and come any time you need me . . . I'll do whatever you want me to do."

"Thanks, Dad," Scott replied quietly. "I want you to tell Mom."

Tell Mom! Yes, of course, I would have to tell Wanda. But how was I going to tell my wife that three members of her family were infected with the AIDS virus? I wasn't sure myself what all that meant. Nevertheless, I tried to encourage Scott. "Don't worry, I'll take care of that," I replied, doing my best to sound confident. I assured Scott that I would be praying for him and the family, we said good-bye, and I hung up the phone.

I paced the floor as the news sank in. Our family had faced numerous crises before. As a leader in a major church denomination, I had spent my life helping other people in their crises. But this was different. The word *crisis* couldn't contain it.

Mechanically, I changed out of my wet clothes as my mind attempted to absorb and assimilate the information I had received. I knelt down and began to pray. I asked God to make it not true. Maybe the tests were mistaken. The transfusions had taken place nearly three years ago. Surely if the problems with the blood were that serious, they would have surfaced before now. But as I prayed, I received no indication in my spirit that meted the nation into the Great Depression. Five babies from our neighborhood died during that plague of scarlet fever. I came close to being the sixth.

I still remember the yellow sign nailed to the door of our house, warning that our family was quarantined. For several weeks, I was confined to a bedroom, along with my mother, and the door was kept shut at all times. Not even my dad was allowed to enter the room. The door to a second bedroom was nailed shut as well. Dad had to climb into a window to come and go. Through my fever, I could hear Dad calling from the other room, asking me how I was doing.

At the height of my sickness, Mother sat at my bedside for hours, rubbing my hands with oil because the doctor had said I might lose the use of them even if I survived. In the next room, we could hear my dad praying, pleading for the life of his only child. Dad had been running away from God's call to preach the gospel. That was how we had gotten to Detroit from our home in Hope, Arkansas in the first place. Dad promised God that if he would spare my life, Dad would return south and preach God's Word. God did and Dad did. It was a major turning point in the life of my family, but the painful memories of that forced isolation made an indelible impression on me.

Now, as the plane whisked me toward Dallas, I wondered if Scott, Lydia, Matt, and Bryan might have to endure a similar quarantine. If so, how could such an isolation be done nowadays? And how could they be shielded from the angry outcries of neighbors, or the dangerous devices of demented individuals who sought to deal with the disease by burning down the homes of the afflicted . . . with the diseased inside?

I also wondered how the family's church fellowship would respond to the news that AIDS was among them. Scott was minister of education at the First Christian Church of Colorado Springs. He was an effective minister and the congregation loved him. Nevertheless, I played out in my mind possible scenarios of the church's reaction, whether or not they would rally around Scott and his ailing family, or recoil in fear.

Most of all, I grappled with the difficult task of telling Wanda the tragic news. I prayed that I could somehow break it to her gently, in a way that would not devastate her. Our family always thought of Wanda as fragile. She had suffered emotional illnesses in the past, which caused our apprehension. Subsequently, my three sons and I always tried to protect her from traumatic events or news. But there was no way I could protect her from this.

I opened my eyes and stared aimlessly out the airplane's small window. The sky was blue above the clouds; it always is. But a thick layer of haze separated the heavens from the earth. The "why" and "how" questions pummeled my faith in the God who rules the earth from above the clouds.

"God, why have you allowed this to happen?"

"Lord, you can do anything. You could have prevented this disease. Why didn't you?"

"Why us? Why this? Why now? Why? Why? Why?"

The God above the clouds was silent, so I knew I was asking the wrong questions. I moved on to mull over the "how" questions.

"How could this have happened?"

"What did we ever do to 'deserve' this?"

"How had my family gotten into this mess . . . ?"

TWO

HOMEGROWN RELIGION

As I THOUGHT of Lydia, Matthew, and Bryan, all condemned to die because of this new mystery disease called AIDS, I realized how radically different our world was from the time I was a boy. When I grew up, we didn't worry about AIDS—the disease did not even exist.

Many people claim to have grown up in the church. I actually did.

The building on the corner of McKinney and Routh streets in Dallas is now the Hard Rock Cafe. When I was growing up, however, it was home and church and a place where I discovered the presence of God in my life. It was where I began a lifestyle that emphasized the importance of relationships. My love and expectations for the church, my understanding of roles to be played by religious leaders, and my expectations of what the Father can and will do in our lives all had their beginning in that tiny house/church. My dad, Earl Allen, was the pastor of that church.

God had first spoken in Earl Allen's spirit, calling him to preach, when he was a teenager on an Arkansas farm. Earl had resisted the idea because preachers were so poor. Most preachers he knew couldn't support their families, and as one of eight children, Earl knew he had to find a way to make some money. A gifted athlete, he was the first in his family to finish high school. He took some extension courses and became a schoolteacher and a coach.

When Earl Allen married Edna Ray, they were the talk of Hope, Arkansas. He was almost six-feet-two-inches tall and she was four-feet-eleven! She was sixteen and he was twenty-three. She was the public speaker, performing at the community programs. He was the hard-bodied athlete with a slight stutter in his speech. By the time I was born, Dad had decided to put off preaching in hopes that he could serve God some other way.

Dad couldn't see himself as a stuttering preacher, but he knew he could play basketball! He could teach other people to do it, too. He was offered a job as player-coach by a pipeline company, if he would move to Detroit. In 1928, sports often were funded by businesses rather than by educational institutions. Dad accepted the job and as he was swept up in the move, he set aside things of the Spirit. But he had not reckoned with the faith and faithfulness of his lovely, eloquent, and absolutely determined bride. In Detroit, Mom found a place of worship for herself and her baby. She also prayed for Dad, and for something to bring him to his senses.

Something did. In 1929 when the stock market crashed, the first thing cut from the floundering business was its basketball team, coach and all. Dad finally found a job with a life insurance company, selling nickel policies door-to-door. Five cents down and five cents a week. My dad, the stutterer, was making a living by talking!

It was not until my battle with scarlet fever, and Dad's "bargain" with God, that we returned south to Dallas. Dad spent the next few years struggling to keep our family alive. By the time Dad decided to step out in faith and start a church, I was eight years old. We went to look at the house on McKinney Avenue. It was two stories, with a front porch and a decent-sized yard. Upstairs provided room enough for the three of us to live. Someone offered us some chairs and a piano, and our dream of a house/church became a reality.

Dad quit his insurance job. He had three cents in his pocket and no assured income. The rent on the house was fifty-five dollars a month, and no denominational group helped us make the payments.

As a family, we often knelt and prayed, asking God to provide for us and take care of us. During the two years we lived in that building, we never missed a payment or a meal. Sometimes answers to our prayers came in simple ways. One day, Dad called a meeting of the family. He said, "We are here to serve God. He has led us to start this church, but we don't have anything to eat today. We don't have any money to get something to eat. The Bible says, 'Once I was young and now I am old. I have never seen the righteous forsaken or his seed begging bread.' Mother, do you believe in prayer?"

Mother replied, "Yes I do."

"Jimmy, do you believe in prayer?"

"Yes sir, I do," I answered, a bit tentatively but truthfully.

"Then we are going to ask God to give us something to eat today." We got on our knees. One at a time, we asked God to provide something for us to eat. It was nine o'clock in the morning.

A little while later, Evelyn Taft came by. Evelyn was a young woman who was attracted to our street mission and regularly attended the church. She knocked on the front door with one hand as she held a one-pound bag of pinto beans in her other hand. "I have these beans," she said, "and I don't have a place to cook them. If you will cook them, I'll come back later and eat them with you."

Mother laughed as she gratefully poured the beans out on the top of the table. She found a piece of salt pork and some corn meal, so we had corn bread and pinto beans to eat that night, with water to wash it down.

Living in the church on McKinney Avenue, I learned something of the immediacy of God's provision for his children. I also learned he sometimes answers prayer with a pound of pinto beans.

Starting a church from scratch meant taking neighborhood door-to-door surveys. Dad worked on one side of the street and I took the other. I was eight years old.

One hot summer day, we went door-to-door at mid-morning to beat the sweltering Dallas heat. Watching Dad inviting people to church stirred my courage. I knocked on the door of a two-story house. The door was opened by a large lady in a blue wraparound dress with huge red flowers on it. Her black hair had streaks of gray shining through it. On her nose rested thick reading glasses. She peered down ominously, as she listened to me give my spiel about the church my family had started. Finally, she exclaimed, "Do they send babies out from that church?"

I replied, "Lady, if you'll come help us, we won't have to do that."

Years later when my election as president of the Southern Baptist Convention made the news, I received a letter from Stella Simms. She was living in Arizona and she recalled our visit on her front porch. She declared that there had never been a time since that day when she was not involved in helping a mission church get started.

I was twelve years old when I heard the call to preach. No doubt, living in the shadow of my parents' faith had a lot to do with it. Prior to my call, I had been seriously, though spasmodically, sharing with my playmates my experience with God and my belief in him. They weren't greatly interested.

I prayed faithfully, and Bible readings were a part of my daily life. Once in a while, I had some personal struggles over matters of conscience, after which I asked for and claimed God's forgiveness. I had just gone through one of those times when the call came.

I attended boys' camp at Latham Springs Encampment near Hillsboro, Texas. It was an adventure. We stayed in rustic cabins, ate in a dining hall, and played ball in the hot Texas sun. Camp baseball was dusty, sweaty, and wonderful. After the games, swimming in the concrete pool fed by the river was even better.

Besides fun and games, the Baptists stressed a strict regimen of religious services to start each day. I went barefoot to the worship service every morning, usually with nothing serious on my mind, and I sat in the back. At the end of the service, we sang a closing song as invitation to boys to come to the altar, either to begin their commitment to Christ as Master of their lives (a commitment I had made), or to confess sin and renew promises made to God (something I had recently done). Not much of significance happened in my heart as the preacher spoke. Yet, one morning as we sang the closing song, I felt a strange yearning to make a deeper response to God. I bowed my head and asked God what he wanted from me.

About that time, a man I did not know stepped from the back of the open-sided tabernacle to stop the singing and say, "I believe there is a boy here who is being called to preach the gospel. I was twelve years old when I first knew I was to preach the gospel."

I knew the man was talking about me.

In Baptist traditions, ministers are expected to surrender to a "call." Without such a call from God, people are not encouraged to choose the pastorate simply as a profession. There is supposed to be a conviction that God is guiding a person into full-time ministry. All true Baptists take seriously their duty to share and explain the gospel, but the call to preach goes beyond personal evangelism. The call is a gift to be received from God alone. The sharpening of one's communication skills can come with experience and training, but the call cannot be manufactured.

Answering the tugging at my heart, I responded to God's call. I went down to the front of the tabernacle and knelt at the altar. I was one of several boys making a public decision that morning. This happened routinely. No one made much of it. But it was not an ordinary day in my life, nor was this merely an emotional jag or a superficial commitment. Many times in my life's journey, I have gone back to that moment and that sense of mystery at being chosen by God. It has been affirmed

again and again. God did something in my life that
morning that caused me to forgo my teenage vocational
daydreams. Even when I struggled against it in my early
adolescence, I knew that I was chosen.

One of the most subtle lessons learned from growing
up in a house/church was the role and relationships of
leaders within the religious community. It came not
from instruction but from osmosis. Pastors and their
family members were to be examples. Our weaknesses
or problems we kept private. We didn't call them
secrets, but they were well-guarded nuggets of information nonetheless. While we cared for others who had
problems, we kept quiet about any problems of our
own. We were to take our troubles to the *Lord,* not to
the *Lord's people.* I wasn't to tell anyone about our
needs . . . or my wants. I was to keep my head high
and clothes clean. I might have only one change of
clothes, but it was family business.

I also learned that people in ministry were to be
friendly to everybody, but to have no favorites. Welcomed into each circle in the congregation, we were to
belong to none. Close friends were best found outside
the congregational family. We didn't think of it as being
artificial or hypocritical. It was the rhythm of the public
life, and the private personality of pastoral leadership.
We were led to believe that there is a natural gap between leaders and followers. Secrets were okay, so long
as they were not a cover-up for unacceptable behavior.

The fishbowl was home to me. I soon discovered
personal retreats into the presence of the Father were
a sturdy lifeline, while the human network I found
fragile.

THREE

SECRET
COMPANIONS

A BIT OF ARKANSAS wisdom treasured by our family is: "You don't make friends . . . you discover them." As I moved through life I collected evidence that this maxim is true. Those companions are essential. This journey is too rough to go it alone.

I was a senior at Howard Payne University in Brownwood, Texas when I first saw the woman with whom I would share my life. A young student minister, I had preached at the 7 A.M. worship service on campus, and was eating breakfast at the canteen when I heard an infectious laugh. I wheeled around on my stool to see a cute, black-haired, five-foot-two-inch bundle of energy. I immediately made it my business to find out the young woman's name—Wanda Massey.

It was 1947, and I had just turned twenty years old. I was busy trying to finish college and hold down a job as assistant pastor and youth director at the First Baptist Church in Dublin, forty-five miles from Brownwood.

Wanda had grown up in Wichita Falls where her father owned an automobile business. No one in her family of automobile dealers much liked the idea of her marrying a preacher. One of her uncles was so intent on keeping her away from me that he offered to pay for her to attend a university in faraway South Carolina. Fortunately, she refused.

Soon Wanda came to campus every morning for the devotional services that I led. I finally received her family's stamp of approval when Wanda's Uncle Luther, the patriarch of the family, came to hear me preach in a revival service in Beaumont. Afterwards, he called Wanda's dad and said, "Well, Bill, if she's got to marry a preacher, at least she is marrying a good one."

With studying and preaching, I was so busy that it was difficult for us to have a normal romance. On our first date I took her to a funeral home and a radio station. She had never been behind the scenes of either one. And I needed to see my friends who were operating them. Besides, at that point in my personal discipline, I thought movies too "worldly." It wasn't an auspicious beginning, but we laughed our way through it.

In fact, it was Wanda's humor, candor, and caring that attracted me to her. She was a drama major and a talented comedienne. While I usually finished second on the college debate team, Wanda won intercollegiate honors in after-dinner speaking contests.

After graduating from Howard Payne, I enrolled at Southwestern Baptist Theological Seminary in Fort

Worth. While working on my master's degree, I took a
job as director of Texas Royal Ambassadors, a Baptist
organization similar to the Boy Scouts, except that it
trains young men to participate in Baptist missions activities. On weekends, I worked in the Dallas office,
and in the summer, I worked at the boys' camps. As
director of the camps, I had the opportunity to preach
in pulpits all across the state. It was great training for
my future roles in our denomination.

Wanda and I married after the final camp in August
1949, only two days after her nineteenth birthday.
Wanda was determined to be a good pastor's wife, but
like most minister's wives, she underestimated the cost.
At church, Wanda was the same person she always had
been—candid and open, someone who followed her
impulses. Nothing in her background prepared her for
the hidden, unspoken ways of the church. She did not
know how to be a selective friend; how to be in the
public's eye, and yet maintain a strict code of privacy;
how to carefully handle ticklish people and contro-
versial issues. To Wanda, friendships were genuine,
wholehearted, and cherished. She led with her heart,
reaching out and responding with authentic feeling to
everyone she met. Wanda was either on or off; hot or
cold; she either loved something or hated it, but she
was never indifferent.

As I finished work on my master's degree, Wanda
and I felt we were ready for our first full-time pastorate.
We went to "preach in view of a call" at a Baptist
church in Van Alstyne, Texas, a tiny town of 1,600
people, fifty miles north of Dallas. Driving into town
early one Sunday morning, we passed rolling hills covered with cotton, maize, and oats. We stopped at the
only traffic light in Van Alstyne. On the corner stood a
solid brick church that had been built in 1929. I sat in

my car, impressed by the building but mentally trying to swat away the butterflies in my stomach. I was only twenty-three years old. Would the stoic, hardworking, rock-ribbed farmers who attended that church accept me as their pastor?

While the congregation debated that question after the service, Wanda and I waited in the dank basement. I was relieved when a small group came and told us they had voted to ask us to come as pastor and wife. Later, I found out that eight people had voted against us. But at that moment, I wasn't concerned about the opposition.

Wanda took the town like she had taken the university—by storm. I was still commuting to classes in Fort Worth eighty miles away, but Wanda stayed in touch with the people of the church. I soon realized that people loved her, and respected me. All through our lives, in every church we have served, the people have called her *Wanda,* and me *Reverend* or *Doctor Allen.*

I immediately set out trying to change things at that little church, and quickly learned a lesson in pastoral patience. The first thing I tried to change was a mural over the baptistry. During the 1930s an itinerant artist had painted the mural, depicting a river lined with grotesque looking trees, in sickly hues of greens and brown. I thought it had to go. The people thought otherwise. When I left for my next pastorate, the mural was still there.

I was happy to be pastoring in Van Alstyne, but I sensed a desire to do more, to win more people to the Lord, to grow larger congregations, to build bigger and more extravagant churches. To satisfy my thirst for growth, I went out into the countryside and preached in places where other churches had folded. My own congregation grew, but I was frustrated, eager to go someplace bigger.

Wanda, on the other hand, was happy. Our first son, Michael, was born while we were in Van Alstyne. Wanda labored for twenty-three hours to bring Michael into the world, and the birth was a difficult one. At first, our blonde, blue-eyed baby boy looked completely healthy. But later, Michael was diagnosed with paranoid schizophrenia, a mental disorder that has brought chaos to his life and ours. Doctors told us that the long and difficult birthing process may have contributed to his condition. Perhaps so, but the evidence of paranoid schizophrenia did not show itself at first, and in those halcyon days, we simply enjoyed Michael. With Wanda's efforts, our home—as well as the dark, musty church nursery—was transformed with bright, cheerful colors.

Soon a larger church in the town of Wills Point wanted us to come to them, and I broached the idea to Wanda. She resisted at first, then agreed. Once in Wills Point, she adjusted quickly and made the place her own.

Our other two sons were born there: Skip (born Stephen) in 1953, and Scott in 1956. Both boys were to become major players in the secret our family carried in the 1980s.

It was also in Wills Point that I first noticed Wanda's mood swings. The price she paid for being publicly on stage was a dark depression that did not emerge fully until years later.

Looking back, I now realize I was as much a part of the problem as the solution. I was obsessed with God. My relationship with God is the primary one of my life. Living with a man with any kind of obsession—even with God—is not easy. It created pressure on Wanda of which I was only dimly aware. As the first family of the church, Wanda and I were committed to living in a fishbowl. I was acclimated to it, but for Wanda, our life in parsonages became a kind of black hole, luring her in, but not letting her out.

Next to Wanda, the other significant partnership I struck up in my twenties was with Luke Williams, a fellow Baptist I met at a boys' camp the summer after my first year in seminary. Growing up an only child in the inner city, I had always wanted a brother. The sense of aloneness I felt as a kid wasn't imaginary; it was reality. I coped with it by learning to box. Boxing taught me how to defend myself on the streets, but it never replaced my longing for a brother.

Then I met Luke—a short, compact, muscular man. One morning a busload of boys pulled up to the encampment grounds near Denton, Texas. The name Midway Baptist Church, Fort Worth was scrawled on the side of the bus. Luke Williams was the counselor in charge of the boys. Born in the mountains of north Georgia, Luke was reared as a Methodist. He became a Baptist when he married his wife, Joyce, and entered the Baptist seminary in Fort Worth. He was twenty-four years old when I met him on the first day of Baptist boys' camp.

I stepped on the bus, clipboard in hand, baseball cap on my head, and whistle around my neck. "Welcome," I told the boys. "Welcome to a camp in which we have no rules!"

The boys cheered.

"I mean it," I continued. "All we ask is that you do what's fair and right," I explained to a hushed crowd. "Now let me help you figure out what is fair and what is right. You can stay up all night every night if you want to do so. However, it would not be fair to keep anybody else up. It would be unfair to cause your counselor to lose sleep. Therefore, if you want to stay up all night, you just lie in your own bed, totally quiet, with your eyes open."

By the time I'd finished the definition of fair and right, the bus was completely quiet. Luke later laughed and said that he knew right then that he had met a regular martinet.

Luke became a minister of education, putting his organizational skills to use in churches all over America. His singing voice was deep and clear, and for a time he also served as choral director of a church.

Luke and I served in different churches and communities for nineteen years, but in 1968 our vocational paths joined, and we became a team. Luke already was employed at the First Baptist Church in San Antonio when I went there as pastor. The chemistry was right between us. Luke was quiet and detailed. I was noisy and full of ideas. He was the implementor, and I was the innovator. Together we energized a giant downtown church, launched an international missions program through the Southern Baptist Convention, and founded the ACTS satellite television network.

Luke's greatest gift was organization. When the movie *Cool Hand Luke* came out, the title so typified Luke's unflappable nature that it became his nickname. He had more patience than I could ever muster. He often said, "Never laugh at any idea in a brainstorming time." And he wouldn't. Instead, he listened and thought, probing possibilities for practical steps. He would say, "You preachers have an unusual capacity for vision. That's God's way of using you. I listen and see if we can make the vision come true."

In the informal atmosphere of the midweek prayer

services of our church, Luke brought his notebook and pen. He said, "I listen closely to what you tell the people. That's how I find out my job assignments for the near future." He demanded no spotlight. Instead, he got joy out of accomplishing tasks.

Luke was so private it was sometimes scary. Ask a direct question, you'd get a direct answer. On the other hand, if you didn't ask a specific question, no information was offered.

We played tennis together. We prayed together. We laughed together. Next to Wanda, Luke Williams became my best friend in the world. Like Wanda, Luke had a terrific sense of humor. While hers was verbal, his was quiet, subtle, and wry. When the thermostat in the church broke, and people complained that it was too hot or too cold, he nodded and told them, "Well, thank you. Let's just turn the cooling (or the heat) up some." Then he would turn it up. I watched him for years turn that broken thermostat up or down. Only the two of us knew it wasn't connected to anything, but people felt much better when "something was done about it."

Luke and I shared a ministry and similar points of view. Later, we also shared two grandsons. His daughter Lydia and my son Scott became husband and wife. In time, we also shared the burden of the secret. The stress of carrying that secret would eventually become more than Luke's good heart could take.

FOUR

SCOTT—
OUR FIGHTER

My YOUNGEST SON, Scott, has been highly competitive all of his life. He had to be a fighter; he was born into a hostile environment. Almost as a foreshadowing of things to come in his life, the joy and excitement we felt at Scott's birth was obscured by concern over a blood-related, deadly disease.

Infectious hepatitis was a mystery disease in the 1950s. Ironically, Wanda was exposed to it through a shot at the doctor's clinic in our small town. She fought her way back to health, and a year after her hepatitis was in remission, Wanda became pregnant with Scott. The pregnancy was problem-ridden from the beginning, and due to complications, Wanda's doctor decided to do a Caesarean section during the seventh month. It was uncertain what effect Wanda's hepatitis might have on the baby, but when Scott was born, it was only natural that his yellowed skin was at first thought to be hepatitis-related. No one knew at the time that Scott also had a critical Rh-factor blood problem. A faulty laboratory report masked the fact that the Rh factor was the trouble. Eventually, the doctors discovered the problem, but the late diagnosis meant several days of delay in treatment.

Our baby was dying the day I drove him the fifty miles from Wills Point to Baylor Hospital in Dallas. Wanda was lying helpless and hurting with no new baby to nurse in the Wills Point clinic, so my mother accompanied me to Dallas, carefully and prayerfully attending to Scott all the way to the hospital. As I walked up the steps of the massive white building, carrying Scott in my arms, I felt a profound wave of grief. We were there to see if the newly tried blood exchanges at this major blood center might save our son. We had no reservations about accepting donors' blood in those days. Our baby needed blood-work, and this was a place we could have it done. Nevertheless, I knew the prospects were not good. I found myself planning his funeral as I looked at him, lying listless and yellowed in his infant's hospital crib. He remained in that condition for nearly six weeks.

Life has a way of going in circles from generation to generation. My father's prayers—pleading for my life when, as a three-year-old, I lay quarantined and racked with scarlet fever—were a mirror image of my pleading with God for Scott's life during those six weeks on the children's ward of Baylor hospital. Now it was my turn. I experienced firsthand the helplessness and agony of a father's love in a situation where apart from God's intervention there is no hope.

I was profoundly impacted by being on the children's ward of that hospital. It became a world of weary waiting while Scott was in neonatal care fighting for his life. Time hung heavily, as grief gradually, imperceptibly, was replaced by anxious hope.

During the monotonous waiting periods, I visited a cute, black-haired, four-year-old boy in the room across the hall from Scott. The bright-eyed youngster quickly let me know that his name was Johnny. Johnny was in the hospital for his fourth major surgery. He had been born with only a stump where one leg should have been. Besides the missing limb, Johnny had all kinds of malformations in his intestinal system. He was what would later be described as a thalidomide baby.

As I looked at Johnny, I could not help thinking of my own three boys.

I said, "Johnny, I have a little boy your age. His name is Mike."

Johnny stuttered, "D . . . d . . . does Mike wear cowboy boots?"

"Oh, yes, he wears cowboy boots all the time. His mother and I have to wait until he's asleep to take them off," I replied with a smile.

"Th . . . th . . . the doctor says that after this surgery, I'm going to wear *two* cowboy boots!"

I forced myself not to look at Johnny's stump as I blinked back tears. After a moment I stepped out in the hall and walked to the window; I stood there and thanked God that my little boys could wear two shoes, not just one.

That very day the doctor brightened my family's hopes by reporting that the tide had changed for Scott. One more transfusion probably would do it. Our baby was going to live! During blood exchange after blood exchange, while we waited to see if Scott's tiny body would respond, a conviction grew in my spirit that God had something special to do in and through this boy's life. I regarded the doctor's words as confirmation of what I was sensing. What a relief it was when Scott responded positively to the treatments! Another wave of relief came when we discovered that the ordeal had not adversely affected his brain.

The only remaining negative effect of Scott's difficult introduction to this world was a scrawny, twisted foot. Prior to this point, we hadn't paid much attention to the little limb because of our concern for his blood. Now the doctors fashioned a metal brace to correct the bone. Scott only had to wear the brace at night, but it looked so painful that four-year-old Michael couldn't stand it. Mike would slip into Scott's room at night and unscrew the brace. He couldn't bear his "pretty baby brother" having to go through that pain.

After a few weeks, the problem with Scott's foot was corrected, but concerns over his blood count continued to crop up. We went through anxious months of testing for what was diagnosed as borderline leukemia, and Scott was plagued by low-grade fever for two years. Wanda and I held our breath, hoping and praying that he would be well. Deep inside, however, I felt a peaceful assurance that Scott would be all right. After all, God had some special work for him to do. . . .

Besides, Scott was a fighter. From somewhere in the Allen gene pool, Scott picked up my adrenaline-driven energy. Small and quick, he was far better coordinated than I had been. Of course, competing with two older brothers toughened him, too. Yet Scott always had a soft, sensitive side, as well.

One Halloween night, when Scott was three years

old, the boys got ready to go trick-or-treating. Scott chose to masquerade as Casper, the Friendly Ghost. Towheaded, freckles dotting his nose, dressed in a much-too-large white sheet, Scott was a Kodak moment as he prepared to scare the socks off everyone. But when he saw his own reflection in the sliding glass door, he spooked. He turned and ran into my arms crying, "Daddy, Daddy, I'm scared of my own boo!" That may have been temporarily true, but Scott grew up to be scared of nothing.

He was the smallest kid in his class on his first day in school. With his butch haircut and lunch box in hand, he looked too small to be starting first grade. Wanda and I were concerned about whether Scott could take care of himself at school. We needn't have worried.

A big, clumsy, fourth-grader had been terrorizing the younger children during recess. The teachers were perplexed about how to stop his attacks. When one day he started in on Scott, the school bully quickly discovered that he had run into a ripsaw. Scott was all over him. Crying and running for safety, the bully suddenly decided to change his ways. When I heard the story, I changed some of my ways, too—I stopped worrying about Scott's size.

During Scott's teenage years, he was athletic, quick of mind, and exuberant in spirit. Still, there was little evidence in his adolescence that this boisterous, wild-haired blond would become a preacher. He was rowdy and rebellious. Scott's rebellions were matched by my efforts to exert my fatherly influence to "fix" them. Both of us were engaged in a losing cause.

I recognized Scott's determination to do things his way. I had experienced some of the same drives in ado-

lescence, but my life was tempered with a spiritual definition and dedication that Scott had not yet developed.

Scott's natural tendency toward rebellion was exacerbated by the frequent absences of his parents during his
crucial junior high and high school years. We had
moved to San Antonio, where I was busy leading a
great congregation of over seven thousand people at
the First Baptist Church. After serving in San Antonio
for about a year, I was elected vice president of the
Texas Convention of Southern Baptists. The following
year, I was elected president of the Texas Convention,
providing leadership for more than two million Southern Baptists in the Lone Star State, while continuing to
pastor First Baptist in San Antonio.

I did my best to balance my church leadership responsibilities with my priorities of being a good
husband to Wanda and a good father to my boys. I
constantly juggled my pastoral schedule with the boys'
athletic games, school programs, and plays. Nevertheless, the toll taken upon my family showed up most
frequently as a lack of both quality and quantity of time
spent with my wife and children. Wanda was accustomed to my multi-track, pastoral lifestyle, but Mike
and Skip were completing high school and getting
ready to leave the family nest, and Scott was completing junior high and about to enter high school. If ever
there was a time when they needed both Wanda and
me to be there for them, it was then.

Unfortunately, I was busy building a great church,
and Wanda was beginning to have troubles of her own.

While I served as vice president of the Texas Convention, Wanda started experiencing severe migraine
headaches. The migraines created swelling in her brain
that resulted in excruciating pain. She plunged into

prolonged and deep periods of depression, to the point of displaying suicidal tendencies.

At first, her doctor attempted to treat her with a prescription drug known as Talwin. The doctor assured us that the drug was not addictive. He was wrong. Wanda became dependent upon the drug almost immediately. Yet without the medicine, Wanda's headaches became so debilitating and her depression so intense it was necessary for her to be hospitalized. We checked her into Timberlawn Hospital in Dallas. Timberlawn's treatment technique required a lengthy stay, but none of us imagined it would be fourteen months before Wanda could come home to us.

I traveled back and forth between my church responsibilities in San Antonio and visitation with Wanda in Dallas. It was a four-hour trip by car, or about a one-hour flight by airplane. The church rallied around us and helped meet my family's needs, as well as the many demands for ministry. We had an outstanding staff of over twenty-five people, and they carried the ball for me. I was the quarterback, but they ground out the touchdowns, one inch at a time. The administrator who kept everything flowing smoothly was Luke Williams.

Similarly, at the Texas Convention level, I had an indefatigable group of coworkers who gave of themselves to help me lead our denomination. They were aware of Wanda's condition, and everyone pitched in a little extra to help me compensate. As on the local level, I was the pacesetter, but my staff made the ministry happen.

Ironically, both the local church and the state convention grew by leaps and bounds during that time. Despite my dark days and difficult nights, I felt a sense of fulfillment. God blessed my ministry efforts and I learned that God often chooses to minister to people out of our weaknesses rather than our strengths.

In the meantime, I was determined to be father and mother to the boys . . . especially to Scott, as he entered a crucial period in his life. I tried hard, but I knew I was failing to keep him in the fold. It was a special sorrow for me to watch him slipping away from our close family relationship, into a fog of drug and alcohol usage.

Scott was not a heavy drug user, but even his experimentation was enough to cause more chaos in his life and that of the other family members. Furthermore, Scott's bizarre behavior due to use of alcohol created heartache for all of us. For generations, my family's experience with alcohol had produced the maxim, "Allens can't drink." As a lifelong abstainer, I have not tested the validity of the statement, but over the years, I have observed numerous aunts, uncles, and other Allen family members who have proven the maxim to be true. Scott was no exception.

When Wanda finally returned home, Scott's behavior improved, but he remained wayward. Nevertheless, having Wanda back at the center of our family, able to function now that the doctors had discovered the chemical imbalance in her brain and were treating it with proper medication, gave Scott a sense of security.

Mike and Skip had graduated by this time. When it was Scott's turn to choose a college, he decided on Texas Lutheran, in Seguin. He spent a year at that college, and enrolled in several religion courses, but he was living recklessly. He dawdled away his first year of college by drinking, dating, and defying anyone who attempted to settle him down. Nevertheless, like the Hound of Heaven in Francis Thompson's famous poem by the same title, the Spirit of God continued to pursue Scott.

The turning point came in dramatic fashion.

One night at about 11 P.M., I received a telephone call from the emergency room at Northeast Baptist Hospital in San Antonio.

"Are you Scott Allen's father?" an emotionless voice asked.

"Yes, I am."

"We have him here. He has been in an automobile accident."

As Scott had driven aimlessly up and down country roads, trying to think, a drunk driver had swerved into his lane at a high rate of speed and hit Scott's car head-on. Apparently, by a last-second lunge, Scott narrowly missed being crushed by the car's steering wheel, but his reflexes weren't fast enough to prevent him from hurtling headlong into the windshield.

I rushed across town to the hospital. I raced into the emergency room and was met by an unforgettable sight. Blood was everywhere. Scott's face was in shreds, his forehead sliced away and hanging by a thread of skin. I thought sure he was dying.

But Scott survived. Once again, God spared his life. Coupled with my feelings of overwhelming gratitude, I couldn't help but wonder again what great thing God wanted to do through this young man's life.

Scott sensed it, too. One sunlit day after the crisis was over and Scott was well on his way to recovery, I was in his hospital room talking with him. Suddenly, Scott said, "Dad, I died."

I nodded. "You were very close to it," I replied.

"No, I really died. I was gone. I left my body. I could see what was happening, but I was dead," Scott answered emphatically. Something about the way Scott related his experience told me that he had not been hallucinating. I didn't quite know how to respond to this dramatic tale, but I believed my son was telling me the truth.

This eerie experience changed the direction of Scott's life. His attitude changed for the better. He became more sensitive to spiritual things. He was more conscientious about his academic studies. He spent more time talking with the family. The accident and Scott's injuries had been horrible, but I recognized that God was using the ordeal for good. I identified with the feelings of the father in the story of the prodigal son (Luke 15:11–32). My boy had come home.

Several weeks later, after the plastic surgeon had repaired his face and his body was healing, Scott was scheduled to return to the hospital for the removal of one last scar over his eyebrow. He decided to forgo the procedure and leave the scar as a constant reminder. "I'll remember this near-death experience every time I look in a mirror," he explained.

As he followed through on his search for the meaning of God's touch in his life, Scott became a religion major at Baylor University. He took his studies seriously and as he neared the completion of his undergraduate education, Wanda and I began to breathe a collective parental sigh of relief. We felt that we had weathered the storm, that we had survived the worst attacks our family would ever have to go through. Little did we know that we had merely been in boot camp. The real battles were yet to come.

For the time being, though, our family was happy. Wanda was doing well. After being hospitalized repeatedly for schizophrenia, Mike had attended Texas State Technical Institute, and was working as a carpenter.

Skip had gone to Houston Baptist College for a year, then worked in San Antonio and Dallas, where he could pursue the theatrical work he loved.

Scott was at Baylor and had finally found a sense of purpose in life. Besides that, he was dating Lydia Williams, the devout Christian daughter of my best friend and colleague, Luke Williams. What could possibly go wrong?

FIVE

LYDIA

One Monday morning I met Luke Williams at the church office.

"I talked with my daughter last night," Luke told me matter-of-factly.

I wasn't surprised. I knew Luke's daughter, Lydia, well. I had watched her grow up from the time she was a baby. I had been her pastor in San Antonio since her high school years. Lydia was now a young woman, a nurse, having done her training at Dallas Baptist College. She was doing further studies at Southwestern Seminary in Fort Worth. I also knew the special relationship she had with her daddy. It wasn't strange for Luke to pass along news of Lydia, and I was always glad to hear it. She was like my own daughter.

"Oh?" I replied. "How is my girl doing?"

"I'm not sure," said Luke. "When I called her apartment, your son answered."

"What?" I was shocked. My son, Scott, was a student at Baylor, in Waco. I decided I'd better have a talk with him. I knew that Scott and Lydia had dated, but I did not know that they were getting serious about each other.

Before I talked with Scott, I asked Skip whether he knew if his younger brother and Lydia were in a serious relationship.

"Believe me, Dad," Skip replied, "it's serious."

When Scott and I had a conversation about his relationship with Lydia, I laid the law on him. I loved Scott and didn't want to insult my son, but I also loved Lydia, and I did not want to see her hurt either. I knew that Scott had dated numerous young women while in college, women with whom he had no intentions of carrying on a long-lasting relationship. I didn't want Lydia to fall for Scott, only to have him move on to the next attractive woman he encountered. Besides, as her pastor, I felt a special responsibility for Lydia. I had counseled her through some difficult times during her teenage years. I knew how emotionally fragile she could be.

When I discussed my concerns with Scott, I quickly realized that my fears were without foundation. He and Lydia had fallen in love, and almost before her mother and daddy or Wanda and I got used to the idea of them dating, Scott and Lydia were planning to get married.

The only explanation for it that I could think of was a law of physics: "Opposites attract." While Scott was high-spirited, tightly wound, and a visionary, Lydia was quiet, controlled, and good with details like her father.

More subdued in her mannerisms than her older sister, Virginia, Lydia fought for her own self-worth and style. Things didn't come as easily for her. For instance, her older sister and younger brother found school to be a breeze, but Lydia had to work hard to perform well in her studies. She was not the athletic type, but that did not keep her from participating fully in life. She enjoyed trying anything from skiing to white-water rafting. She had a feminine gentleness, yet she possessed a steel determination.

Lydia was an attractive young woman, petite, with brown hair, and beautiful, penetrating blue eyes. She could appear pixie pretty, but she never gave the impression that she thought of herself as a beauty. She had an intent way of looking at a person with whom she was speaking, as though she thought whatever the person was saying was very important. Actually, Lydia could hear in one ear only, so she had trained herself to listen more closely.

Lydia held a special place in my heart. Over the years, I watched her participate in youth camps and discussion groups, and I was impressed by her honesty. She was not content with glib answers to tough questions. She wanted to know the truth and she was not afraid to confront error where she encountered it in her search. More importantly, she wanted to know God, and was willing to obey and act on what the Bible said.

In fact, at one point, I became concerned about Lydia when, during her late teenage years, she went through a stage of wanting to treat the Bible like a rule book and a contract.

"If I do this, God has to do that," she said during one of our many conversations. I tried to explain to her that God is God and can do whatever he wants. Furthermore, people who put God into that kind of box quickly grow brittle. They break easily. Life and truth are mysteries, and God escapes any effort for us to control him. His promises are true, but they often are fulfilled in his time, not according to our limited ideas of when and how we think God should act. He is not limited to our level of knowledge or our concepts of time.

Thankfully, Lydia soon grew beyond her tight, mechanical interpretations of scriptural truths. Her relationship with the Lord continued to deepen.

What most endeared Lydia to me, however, was not her intellectual grappling with the great puzzles of life, but her practical, down-to-earth compassion. I often referred to her as "president of the wounded bird society." She was always bringing someone to me who needed help. When I visited congregations in Dallas on various occasions during her college days, I often received a call from Lydia: "While you're here, could you see a friend of mine? She's really messed up and needs to talk to someone."

Lydia was sure her pastor would help. The fact that I had walked her through some rough times when she was suicidal as a teenager may have contributed to her confidence in me.

It was no surprise to me that Lydia decided to attend nursing school. She wanted to help suffering people. Her stint at Southwestern Seminary studying missionary nursing melded her faith and her social consciousness into a theologically sound social activism.

She also had a touching adoration for her father. Lydia loved Luke. In her eyes, her dad was a pillar of strength who could solve any problem if you gave him enough time. A tremendous father-daughter empathy existed between the two of them. They were very much alike.

* * *

In 1978, I was elected president of the largest Protestant denomination in the world, the Southern Baptist Convention. But the joy of that great honor paled in comparison to the joy I felt as my son Scott married Lydia, the daughter of my best friend. The wedding took place in the spring, right after the school term. Scott finished his undergraduate work at Baylor, and Lydia took a nursing job in a hospital. The uniting of our two families, first in ministry and now in matrimony, was like a fairy tale. Except in fairy tales, everyone lives happily ever after, and our fairy tale was about to turn into a nightmare.

SIX

THE FATAL TRANSFUSION

SAN FRANCISCO IS about fifteen hundred miles from San Antonio, but in many ways, it is another world. Yet when it came time for Scott to attend seminary, he and Lydia chose to go to San Francisco, to Golden Gate Theological Seminary. In retrospect, when I think of how they got to San Francisco, part of Scott's rationale in making that decision involved me.

I always have been offended by nepotism, the granting of special favors or status simply on the basis of a person's family name. No doubt I conveyed my feelings on the subject to my sons in various subtle, and some not-so-subtle, ways. So, I should not have been surprised when Scott let it be known that he did not want to attend Southwestern Seminary, the largest Southern Baptist seminary in the world, and the academic institution from which I received my masters and doctoral degrees. Since I was now president of the Southern Baptist Convention, Scott did not want to be tagged as "Jimmy Allen's son."

Even at Baylor, he had been extremely low-key about his "access to power." Once I was talking with one of Scott's professors, Dr. James Leo Garrett, a former professor of mine as well, who was now a good friend. In our conversation, I casually mentioned that my son Scott was enjoying Garrett's course.

With surprise on his face, Dr. Garrett asked, "That Allen boy in my class is *your* son? I had no idea!"

No one could ever accuse Scott Allen of benefiting from nepotism.

Still, it frustrated me that Scott wanted to so distance himself from receiving special treatment because he was my son that he would go to Golden Gate in San Francisco. I had assumed that he would attend Southwestern, not simply because I had, but because Lydia had been enrolled there and had completed one year of her studies. Besides, Golden Gate was the smallest of our six Southern Baptist seminaries.

When I probed the reason for Scott's choice, he replied with candor and a touch of humor. "Dad, I want to attend Golden Gate for three reasons. One, they have a great urban ministries program there, and I want to work in some sort of inner-city ministry. Two, Bill Pinson has just become president of Golden Gate, and he is gathering some exciting and outstanding additions to the faculty there."

Scott paused for effect before continuing with a twinkle in his eye, "And three, it is as far away from your seminary—Southwestern—as I can go, and still be in the continental United States!"

I knew Scott was being facetious, but I also recognized the truth in his humor. His decision was not made out of disrespect for me, or animosity toward the academic institution that I loved. His decision was a reflection of his rugged individualism, his determination to make his own mark on this world. I could appreciate that, and I respected him for it.

California fit Scott and Lydia. They both were sensitive, and greatly concerned for and affected by their environment. They loved exploring the natural beauty of California's coastline. The ocean, whales, dolphins, Muir Woods, Big Sur, and the long stretches of pristine beaches all appealed to them, and Scott and Lydia happily answered the call.

Scott was his playful self, while Lydia was the managerial let's-do-it-this-way figure in their marriage. Her nursing job helped pay the bills while Scott completed his education. At first, they lived and worked in the inner city. Out of their apartment, they organized neighborhood groups for discussion and Bible study. Then they discovered Pacifica, a gorgeous community a few miles southwest of San Francisco, perched upon a narrow strip of land overlooking the Pacific Ocean. The beauty of the deep blue Pacific waters off the Northern California coastline is unparalleled. Scott and Lydia moved to the ocean community and quickly became involved in the Pacifica Baptist Church, first as volunteers, then, while Scott was still completing his pastoral studies, as pastor and wife.

Scott's compassionate, caretaker skills emerged and his eloquence developed. His thoughtful jousting with me over theology kept me on my intellectual toes, as Scott matured into an excellent pastor. His balloon of idealism, however, was rudely punctured when Scott had to deal with the sometimes tenuous balance between ministering to people and the frustrating realities of institutional religion. Scott committed himself to helping hurting people rather than seeking religious "political" power. Lydia, too, continued to grow in her practical ministry and leadership roles. The young couple took seriously the ethical issues of their faith, and sought to help in every opportunity that presented itself.

Once, for example, Lydia accompanied me to Washington for an official dinner with the president. As the leader of the Southern Baptist Convention, I was invited to the White House from time to time during the administration of Jimmy Carter to consult with the president. President Carter was, after all, one of our best known Baptist deacons.

A call from the White House with an invitation to a dinner event came while I was visiting Scott and Lydia in California. Wanda couldn't go, so I asked Lydia if she would like to be my dinner companion. As we greeted President and Mrs. Carter, Lydia could not resist speaking urgently to the president about a meeting she had recently attended on hunger problems in Africa. Lydia suggested the president look into the matter.

President Carter responded politely and sincerely.

Later I said, "Lydia, don't you know that social occasions like that are not times for serious discussions on national policy?"

Her reply was typically Lydia. "I figured I would have just one time in my life to talk personally with the president of the United States, and I wasn't going to waste it."

* * *

Early in the spring of 1982, Lydia became pregnant. Both she and Scott were ecstatic. They threw themselves into learning all they could to prepare for the childbearing process. They were committed to having a natural childbirth, so they read books, attended birthing classes and related activities, and practiced their Lamaze lessons. It was a happy time, with plenty of laughter around their home as the young couple excitedly anticipated their first child.

Despite Lydia and Scott's unbridled joy in preparing to have a baby, troubles began to mount as the pregnancy moved into the seventh month. Lydia began experiencing a severe type of morning sickness. She simply could not hold anything in her stomach for long. Lydia's pregnancy also was troubled by unusual hemorrhaging incidents. Occasionally, she would go into a mini-seizure. As a nurse, Lydia knew how to take care of herself, so she and Scott were not panic-stricken when the seizures occurred. Nevertheless, by October, the problems had intensified, and Scott took Lydia to her doctor.

On the way back from the doctor's office, driving through the afternoon expressway traffic on Highway 101 from San Francisco to Pacifica, Lydia suddenly went into toxic shock. Her face turned ashen white and she gritted her teeth in response to her convulsing body. Scott took one look at Lydia and knew instantly that she was slipping into a coma; he had to do something, and quickly!

Providentially, they approached an exit ramp. Scott glanced at the sign, and to his amazement and relief, he saw that the ramp led directly to St. Mary's Hospital. Scott spotted the hospital, wheeled through the crowded lanes of traffic, jerked the vehicle onto the exit ramp and raced up the road to the hospital. The car careered wildly into the emergency room parking area, where Scott slammed on the brakes and screeched to a stop. He rushed to the emergency entrance, shouting as he ran, "Please help me! My wife is in a coma!"

Emergency personnel hurriedly pulled Lydia from the car, placed her on a gurney, and wheeled her into the treatment room. They immediately administered infusions of magnesium, which saved Lydia's life and the life of her baby. Only three to four minutes had elapsed since Lydia had first gone into shock. Had Scott and Lydia not been so close to treatment, both mother and baby would have died.

The magnesium treatment saved Lydia and the baby, but it created another potential problem. It would be unhealthy to allow the baby to remain in that chemically treated environment for long. Lydia must give birth—soon.

After the initial emergency treatment, Lydia was transferred to the hospital in San Francisco where her doctor was in residence. The doctors there discussed with Scott the possibility of taking the baby by Caesarean section. But because Scott and Lydia desired to have a natural birth if possible, the doctors decided to first try to induce labor. They felt they could safely allow Lydia to deliver the baby naturally. If the baby was not born before nightfall, however, they would have to do the C-section.

Scott telephoned Lydia's parents, Luke and Joyce, and Wanda and me to tell us that Lydia had gone into toxic shock. Scott explained that the doctors were planning to induce labor and they were going to take the baby, one way or the other.

I told Scott that we would be there as soon as possible. Before I hung up the phone, Wanda was packing our suitcases. Wanda and I flew from Fort Worth, Luke flew from San Antonio, and Joyce followed on a later flight, but we all arrived in California that evening while Lydia was still in labor. After we arrived, there was another round of discussions with the doctors concerning the possibility of doing the Caesarean section. Once again, they decided to wait. We huddled in the waiting room and quietly prayed.

Scott ran back and forth from the delivery room to the waiting room, keeping us informed and drawing strength from our encouragement and prayers. We were excited, but deeply concerned, as Scott updated us throughout the late afternoon and on into the early evening. Then, as the California sun slowly slipped below the horizon, Scott shuffled into the waiting room with his latest report. He looked tense.

Lydia was not doing well. After the doctors induced labor, she began hemorrhaging again. It was questionable whether the child would be born alive, and touch-and-go whether Lydia would pull through herself. She had lost a lot of blood and the doctors were giving her a series of transfusions.

We were staggered. After months of joyfully anticipating this occasion, suddenly, what should have been a celebration turned mournful. Joyce, Wanda, Luke, and I continued to pray, while Scott returned to Lydia. On into the night we waited, each hour dragging by as if it dared not end. We all knew that this pregnancy had not been easy; struggles during pregnancy were nothing new to us. But now we were talking about life or death.

*   *   *

Back in the delivery room, the doctors had given Lydia two pints of blood. Around 11 P.M., Lydia was conscious and having close contractions. If she could hold on, the baby would be born at any minute! Her doctor now called for another transfusion to be given.

A nurse picked up a third unit of blood, carefully checked the blood type to make sure it was the same as Lydia's, and attached the container to the pole holding the intravenous lines running to Lydia's arm. The blood appeared to be the same as all the other blood that Lydia had received that day.

But it was not.

The blood in that third unit was tainted with a virus —a relatively new, little-known virus, at the time; a virus now widely known as Human Immunodeficiency Virus, often referred to simply as HIV; the virus that causes Acquired Immune Deficiency Syndrome— AIDS.

The Bible says, "Life is in the blood," but nowadays, death, too, can be in the blood. Little did anyone know that as the lifesaving plasma dripped into Lydia's veins, each drop portended doleful death.

In the flurry of activity in the delivery room that night, it seems doubtful that anyone gave much thought to tainted blood. The hospital was an excellent facility with one of the finest neonatal departments in the nation. Besides, a baby was about to be born!

Within about three minutes after the tainted blood had entered Lydia's body—enough time for the blood to circulate through the baby's system at least seven to eight times—Matthew Benjamin Allen was born.

Scott came out to tell us the news, but he did not speak in the ecstatic tones of a new father. His tone was one of subdued relief that the baby had been born, but neither the child nor Lydia was in stable condition yet. We continued to pray.

It was several hours later when Scott finally came out of the delivery room, and with a fatigued smile, announced, "They both are going to make it."

SEVEN

A NEW LIFE

THE NEONATAL WARD was little Matthew's home for the first six weeks of his life. Because of his premature birth, his intestines were not yet fully functioning. He had to have several surgeries to allow his intestines to work. It was three years before we discovered the full scope of the damage done during those first days of Matthew's life.

Matthew's early movements were sluggish, and the doctors and family members spoke in hushed tones about the possibility of brain damage due to the trauma he had experienced during his birth. I tentatively broached the subject with Scott. "How do you feel about that?" I asked, almost reluctant to speak directly to the issue.

Scott was forthright, as always. "Matt is our baby, Dad, and we are going to love him no matter what."

Lydia remained hospitalized for about three weeks following Matthew's birth. Luke, Joyce, and Wanda stayed at Scott and Lydia's home in Pacifica and Scott stayed at the hospital with his wife. When we were confident that the situation had stabilized, I returned to my speaking schedule. Luke returned to Texas. Our wives remained to help Scott and Lydia.

Wanda and Joyce coped well with the myriad details that had to be attended to in light of the premature birth. The one thing they could not figure out, however, was how to get Scott and Lydia's foreign automobile to function. They could get the car to go forward, but they could not get it into reverse. During their many trips, back and forth from Pacifica to the hospital in San Francisco, to the grocery store, or wherever, they had to maneuver the vehicle so that they could always move forward. Imagine trying to find a parking place in San Francisco where it was not necessary to back up!

Most doctors nowadays agree that breast-fed babies are healthier babies. Lydia's doctors, too, encouraged the new mom to breast-feed her baby, something she wanted to do anyway. Oblivious to the virus that had already attacked Lydia's system, the doctors also were unaware that by breast-feeding her baby, the chances that the HIV would develop into full-blown AIDS in Matthew were about fifty percent higher.

Nonetheless, we were thankful for all the medical marvels performed upon Matthew to help him become established in his young life. Matt, as we took to calling him, showed few signs of being unhealthy during his early days, once his surgeries were completed. He did have a propensity to break out in rashes, but we did not regard that as unusual. We were confident that, given a little time, Matt would be a robust baby.

Upon the completion of Scott's seminary education, he and Lydia were ready for a change. Scott yearned for a simpler lifestyle so in the spring of 1983, he and his family moved to the mountains of Monument, Colorado. Lydia served as a psychiatric nurse in a pediatric hospital in Monument, and Scott served for nine months on the staff of the Ponderosa Baptist Assembly, one of our denomination's encampment and retreat centers. Scott's personality clashed with that of Ponderosa's manager, so Scott recommended a fellow with whom he had gone to seminary for the job, and resigned.

Moving to Colorado Springs, Lydia continued her pediatric nursing career and Scott became minister of education at the First Christian Church, a congregation of the Disciples Church. Although the move entailed stepping out of the Baptist circles in which Scott and Lydia had been raised and were comfortable, they felt it was the right thing to do. Their spiritual instincts proved correct as Scott soon became a popular and productive member of the church's staff.

Meanwhile, Matt progressed marvelously. Every day he seemed to grow stronger and more mentally alert. I knew grandparents were prone to be biased, but I could not help feeling proud of Matt; he was so bright it was amazing! Part of the reason for his mental growth, apart from his God-given abilities, was that Scott and Lydia talked to Matt constantly. Even while he was an infant, they read books to him, sang songs to him, and talked to him almost as though he were an adult.

Wanda often visited the family in Colorado Springs. After several visits, she finally convinced Scott and Lydia that it was okay for them to leave Matt with Grandma and take a night out for themselves. Before Scott and Lydia left the house, they got down on their hands and knees on the floor with Matt. They kissed him and said, "We'll be back in two hours."

It seemed silly to us grandparents, but Scott and Lydia were establishing a pattern with Matt. He always knew where they were and when they would return home. If they could not keep their word to him for any reason, they always called to tell him. As parents, Scott and Lydia felt it was important that Matt know that they would always keep their promises to him. And they did.

When Matt was not yet two years old, Wanda traveled to Colorado Springs to stay with him while his parents went on a ski retreat. One day, Wanda needed some groceries, so she took Matt along with her to the store. As Wanda walked through the supermarket, Matt rode in the shopping cart. He often had watched his mother reading the labels on products, looking for the items' nutritional content, so when he saw a product he recognized, Matt would point and shout, "Grandma, I qualify for that!"

Sure enough, Matt was right; he had his boxes identified and memorized. Rice cakes were fine, certain cereal products were acceptable, but most sugar products were no-no's.

During that same shopping trip, Lydia's personal safety training also was evident. Once, when Wanda stepped out of sight to pick up an item, Matt called,

"Grandma, come back. Someone might come by and get me!"

On the way home from the supermarket, Wanda got her directions slightly confused. Matt gently chided her, "Grandma, are we lost again?" Then he pointed out the proper route home.

And to think we had fretted about whether Matt's difficult birth might have damaged his brain!

EIGHT

BAD BLOOD

IN THE FALL of 1984, unaware that she was carrying the HIV, Lydia became pregnant again. As with Matthew, this pregnancy was hard. Lydia was sick frequently, but this time, because of their previous experience with toxic shock, Scott and Lydia were more cautious. They went for almost weekly checkups so the doctor could keep a close watch on her.

On May 13, 1985, Lydia gave birth to another baby boy, Bryan Caleb. Like his brother, Matt, Bryan was born eight weeks prematurely. It had been another tough delivery for Lydia, and from the moment Bryan was born, his life was in crisis. He was not able to breathe on his own, so the doctors immediately put him on oxygen and in an incubator. Bryan eventually

would outgrow the incubator, but the oxygen tubes remained connected to him all the days of his life.

I flew out to Colorado Springs to see the family the day following Bryan's birth. After our experience at Matt's birth, the tension surrounding Bryan's arrival seemed almost normal. He looked so pathetic as he lay in his incubator, lashed to an oxygen tank with long clear tubes leading to his nose. I nearly wept as I watched his tiny body gently heave, trying so desperately to breathe. Nevertheless, his condition was stable, and for that we were grateful.

When I came back to visit with the family about a week or two later, Bryan was still in the hospital, so Wanda came out to stay with Matt and to help Lydia and Scott. Soon Lydia was back on her feet, although she never felt completely well and robust.

After a few weeks, the doctors allowed Scott and Lydia to bring Bryan home, accompanied by an oxygen tank. He wasn't home long before he had to go back to the hospital for more tests and more medication. Throughout the summer of 1985, the baby was in and out of the hospital repeatedly. The doctors shook their heads. They could not figure out why the medications with which they were treating Bryan were having little or no effect. The doctors had no idea what they were dealing with. . . .

In mid-September, 1985, staff members at a large blood bank gathered together a group of names on their computer printouts. The staffers had been tracking some tainted blood that had been donated by a homosexual man back in the early 1980s. The man had AIDS. Although he was now dead, his blood had been disseminated throughout the blood bank's system, to

hospitals around the country. It was now the thankless task of the staffers to track down where the bad blood had been used, and to notify the people who had received it that they should be tested for HIV immediately. One of the names on the list was LYDIA ALLEN.

What made the staffers' job even more difficult was the growing controversy about HIV in the nation's blood supply. As far back as 1982, evidence existed to indicate that AIDS was transmitted by blood transfusions. In San Francisco, a baby who had no other risk factors contracted AIDS after receiving blood donated by a homosexual man. At least five other documented cases showed the same correlation within the same time period.

Immediately, the Centers for Disease Control in Atlanta notified the American Association of Blood Banks concerning the potential problem. The CDC also presented its evidence at a meeting of pharmaceutical companies that extract and produce the clotting factors in blood used to treat hemophiliacs and others. The essence of their report was: "We have a new disease here—one that can be transmitted through the blood. This virus can be contracted through something that happened several years ago in the person's past. And the virus is not only doubling every six months, it is 100 percent fatal."

Even when the blood banks were aware that some people were infected with the virus through receiving contaminated blood, some blood banks dragged their feet in notifying the victims.

Their reluctance to do more to alert recipients of blood of the potential risk was inexcusable and unconscionable, yet understandable. In the early 1980s, the debate raged over what epidemiologists, doctors, and

scientists then called GRID, an acronym for Gay Related Immune Deficiency, a new disease that was showing up in America mostly among male homosexuals.

Despite the clear-cut evidence that the virus could be spread through the blood supply, as well as through homosexual practices and those of intravenous drug users who shared needles, the American Association of Blood Banks at first refused to screen out blood donated by homosexuals, or even ask questions about a person's sexual conduct. About the only initial change brought about by the news that the virus could infect nonhomosexuals if it got into the blood was a change in the name of the disease from Gay Related Immune Deficiency to Acquired Immune Deficiency Syndrome —AIDS.

At the same time, the homosexual community, most notably in San Francisco, grew in number and political strength. Gays became more outspoken and more public about their sexual preferences. In the mid-1970s, many homosexual men began donating blood to fight hepatitis B, a virus that epidemiologists estimated was then carried by 75 percent of homosexual men in some American cities. Most homosexuals at that time were unaware of HIV or AIDS. They knew a lot of their friends and sexual partners were getting sick, but they did not make the connection between their sexual practices and the high number of unhealthy people in their community.

Partly as a means of achieving greater acceptance in the city, and partly because of their compassion for those who were sick, the gay community in San Francisco and elsewhere sponsored numerous blood drives, urging members to participate by donating blood as often as possible.

Soon blood banks were receiving large numbers of donations from homosexuals. About that time, people in the medical professions noticed a correlation between the blood received from many members of the gay community and the frequent occurrences of unusual, antibiotic-resistant illnesses. One blood bank took the bold step of not accepting blood from homosexuals because of the high risk of contamination. Several other blood banks soon followed that example.

When the blood banks' policy became known, the gay community immediately cried foul. "You are discriminating against us!" they said.

Many blood banks backed away from their no-homosexual-blood policy. They were, after all, in the business of selling blood, and homosexual donors were a major source of the product. At the same time, wanting to show that they were concerned, conscientious citizens, members of the gay community intensified their efforts to give blood. In the process, those donors who had contracted HIV unintentionally were killing people. Ironically, the man whose contaminated blood spread HIV to my family members probably gave blood to be a good citizen.

When the man whose HIV-tainted blood eventually traveled through Lydia's veins died of AIDS, the blood bank searched through its computer files to track where he had donated blood and to whom it was given. Finally, on September 18, 1985, someone at the blood bank had the courage to call Scott and Lydia and tell them the truth.

Lydia answered the telephone that day. In hollow, straightforward tones, the voice on the phone informed her that the donor's blood had been contaminated with HIV, and that she and her family members should be tested immediately. As a nurse accustomed to dealing with other people's delicate situations, Lydia did not crumble at the news. Nevertheless, this was different. This was her family! Lydia instantly recognized that Matt and Bryan and possibly Scott and she herself might be living on borrowed time.

When Lydia told Scott the news, he was devastated, but determined that they waste no time in being tested. The blood tests took about a week to come back.

On September 25, 1985, the report returned, and the results sent the young family into a tailspin: Scott was not infected, but Lydia, Matt, and baby Bryan were HIV-positive. Although it is possible for a person to have the virus and not yet have the symptoms of full-blown AIDS, our family members were not considered healthy carriers. They were headed for AIDS.

That night, after taking a short time to commiserate together and attempt to assimilate the information, Lydia called Luke, and Scott called me in Nashville to tell us that we were now an AIDS family.

NINE

SHARING THE SECRET

THE AIRPLANE on which I traveled from Nashville to Dallas lurched slightly, jolting me out of my thoughts and reminding me of my present need for calm and stability as I prepared to tell Wanda that three members of our family were HIV-positive. I blinked my eyes hard, hoping that I had merely been having a bad dream during the flight, but no matter how tightly I squeezed my eyelids, the surreal images of AIDS would not go away.

"Please fasten your seat belts and return all tray tables to the upright position," a flight attendant requested on the plane's speaker system. "We will be landing at Dallas–Fort Worth International Airport in approximately fifteen minutes."

Fifteen minutes. Suddenly, every minute of life seemed precious. There was no time to be wasted. I must tell Wanda. We had to do something to help our kids. . . .

The plane hit the runway with a bit more bounce than usual, or at least it seemed so to me that day. Despite the airplane's powerful braking system, we rolled down the runway for what felt like miles before we started the trek back to the terminal. The taxi from the runway to the DFW terminal usually takes three to five minutes, but on that day, it felt as though the short trip took an interminable amount of time. I kept shifting in my seat, looking at my watch; I could not wait to get off that plane. Finally, we arrived at the gate.

I had arranged for my secretary, Janice Brake, to pick me up at the airport and drop me off at my office. From there, I drove home by myself, arriving at Wanda's and my Fort Worth townhouse at about eleven o'clock in the morning. All the way home, I asked God for wisdom and grace to handle this conversation. Now as I placed my hand on the doorknob to our front door, I paused long enough to whisper one final, quick prayer, asking God to guide my thoughts and words.

I was unprepared for the sight that met my eyes when I opened that door. Wanda was in a fritz. The dishwasher had broken down, and large puddles of water were all over the kitchen floor. She had called the repair service, and had been told that it would be two or three days before someone could schedule a "non-emergency" service call. The malfunctioning dishwasher may not have been an emergency to the service center, but it certainly was to Wanda!

As soon as I walked into the house, Wanda began relating how frazzled and frustrated she was over the malfunctioning machine. I gently put my arm around her and guided her toward our living room.

"Come, sit here," I said, motioning toward our sofa. "I have something to tell you." Wanda could tell from my somber tone of voice that I had something more serious than the dishwasher on my mind. We sat down together on the sofa.

Nodding toward the kitchen, I began, "You think that is a crisis . . . let me tell you what our real crisis is . . ." I could barely speak. The words stuck in my throat. Very slowly, I told Wanda that Scott had called me in Nashville the night before.

"There is a question about the blood that Lydia received in a transfusion when Matt was born. She and Scott and the boys have been tested and Lydia, Matthew, and Bryan have tested positive for the virus. Scott tested negative—he doesn't have it, but the others do."

Wanda's first response was similar to my own. "Virus? What virus?" she asked. "What does that mean?"

"It's AIDS," I replied quietly. "The three of them have been exposed to AIDS; Scott is the only one who has not."

"AIDS?" Wanda repeated softly.

In an unusual—and perhaps providential—way, Wanda had been prepared ahead of time for our conversation. That week, she had picked up a national news magazine whose cover story was about the new mystery disease, AIDS. For some reason, she had read the cover story word for word, and by the time I arrived home from Nashville, Wanda knew more basic information about HIV than I did. Her awareness did not lighten the shock of the news, but it at least helped her to understand it.

I was surprised at Wanda's emotional composure.

She sat on the sofa, posing questions and offering comments without panic or outburst. She later told me that her calm demeanor was merely an outward reflection of the inner paralysis she felt. What I mistook for courage was shock. Her emotional system had gone on autopilot.

We talked further, prayed briefly, and then sat silently on the sofa and held each other. After a while, Wanda went upstairs to be alone with her thoughts and to pray, and I went into my office to call Luke.

When Luke came on the line, I asked him if he had talked to Lydia. He said that he had, and the two of us talked for quite a while about what we faced. Like me, Luke had recognized the weighty burden of the secret we were carrying. In his conversations with Joyce, and mine with Wanda, we all agreed that the primary issue was: "What could we do to help our children?" For the moment, we simply had to sit tight until we received more information from Scott and Lydia. We knew the situation would be bad, but we had no idea how bad things would be.

That same day, on the Friday following his Thursday night telephone call to me, Scott went to his senior pastor at the church in Colorado Springs to inform him that Lydia and the boys had AIDS. Besides hoping for a measure of concern, counsel, and compassion, Scott and Lydia felt that the pastor would want to inform the parents of children who had been in the nursery and children's ministries with Bryan and Matt. Although Scott and Lydia had no medical reason for suspecting that their children may have passed the infection to other children, their own moral integrity demanded that they at least inform people who may want to have their children tested for the virus.

AIDS was such a new disease, confusion over what it was and how it could be caught was rampant. Nevertheless, especially in light of a delay in learning of their own contamination, Scott and Lydia decided it was better to tell the pastor and hope he would handle the situation properly than to keep the information secret. Their hopes were quickly dashed.

When Scott informed the pastor that Lydia, Matt, and Bryan had AIDS, the pastor asked for Scott's resignation on the spot. Scott did not agree.

Later Scott found a letter on his desk "accepting" his resignation and offering some severance pay until the end of the year. The pastor denies he asked for Scott's resignation. But from Scott's vantage point, the pastor, in effect, fired Scott because his family had AIDS. Over the weekend, the pastor passed the information along to several of his church leaders. The church cabinet had a meeting. At first, it appeared that they might allow Scott to take a leave of absence to deal with the earthshaking news that he had received, but instead, the majority of the church governing body simply accepted Scott's resignation.

Early the following week, Scott cleaned out his desk. Few people in the congregation ever heard the reason Scott left his position at the church. Scott and I talked by phone every day that week, and when I heard of the church leaders' decision, I could hardly believe it. I was puzzled that there was not more of an outcry from the congregation, so I asked Scott, "Everybody didn't want you to leave, did they?"

"No," replied Scott sadly. "There are friends here who want to support us, but I am not going to stay here and tear this church apart. It's better for me to get out."

Lydia worked as a supervising psychiatric nurse in a

children's ward of a local health center. Because she carried the virus, she felt the risk of contaminating somebody else's child was too great to take. She resigned her position immediately. In a matter of days, both Scott and Lydia were unemployed.

At first, they thought they might be able to remain in Colorado and attempt to maintain some normalcy in their lives. Scott could find a job doing something else to support the family. It might have worked, but then Scott and Lydia learned that their confidentiality had been breached. Confidentiality is a highly valued commodity in every area of life, but especially within the medical community and the church community. What can be more sensitive than personal health records and personal problems being exposed to public scrutiny? Apparently, Scott and Lydia's privacy was violated in both of these vulnerable areas.

We suspected that someone who attended the church and also worked in the hospital had spied the family's health records, and had spread the word that the Allens had AIDS. Lydia was asked to remove Matt from the church's day-care center. The family was asked not to return to their church.

Nowadays, it is difficult to imagine the hysteria and paranoia that swept through the community when people found out that AIDS victims were living among them. But in 1985, the fear and suspicion were real. The public was afraid of this new, unknown disease that was compared to ancient plagues. On the other hand, Scott and Lydia's fear of unfair attacks was equally as real. Newspapers, magazines, television, and radio regularly reported incidents of senseless violence and verbal abuse against AIDS victims. Once Scott and Lydia's secret had been made public, moving from the area seemed inevitable.

One of the final straws came when they ordered oxygen to be delivered to their home for Bryan. Word apparently had reached as far as the oxygen suppliers that the Allen baby had AIDS. When the attendant showed up with the oxygen tank, he got out of the truck wearing a diver's helmet and a complete diver's suit! Stumbling along on the dry land of Colorado, fully rigged for undersea diving, he was a grotesque and humorous sight. Breathing like Darth Vadar in Star Wars, he transacted his business and staggered back to the truck.

In the years to follow, mimicking that oxygen attendant's ridiculous actions became a favorite feature of the dark humor sessions that often rescued our family from absolute despair. There was nothing funny, however, when the children moved to Texas, and the same attendant called every oxygen dealer he could find in the Dallas–Fort Worth phone directory to warn them that the Allen family had AIDS.

When it became apparent that Scott and Lydia's church was not going to function for them as "the Church," the mystical, ministering Body of Jesus Christ, I spent whole evenings on the telephone in family discussions. Besides the family's physical well-being, many of my concerns centered around simple logistical issues. What are we going to do? Where are they going to live? How are we going to find a way to support them through this crisis?

As we talked into the evening hours, Scott and Lydia revealed to me that they were thinking about moving someplace where they could be less conspicuous, where their secret could be protected. I immediately offered to have them come to Fort Worth to live with Wanda and me. I knew our modest townhouse would not provide them with much space, but it would give them a home while we searched out other possibilities. Lydia and Scott thanked me and told me they would think about my offer.

A move back to Texas made sense for obvious reasons, not the least of which was that Lydia and Scott could receive much needed support from family members living there. Since 1980, Wanda and I had been living in Fort Worth, where we had moved so I could help pioneer the new American Cable Television System, known as the ACTS television network. Our middle son, Skip, lived nearby in Dallas. Luke Williams maintained an office in our Fort Worth telecommunications center and commuted from San Antonio to help me with the television network. He and Joyce still lived in San Antonio, where Joyce had a satisfying and influential teaching career.

Within six weeks after the call from the blood bank, Scott and Lydia's economic, social, and spiritual support system in Colorado had disappeared. They agreed it would be best for the family to join us in Fort Worth. They stored their furniture, packed their small, movable belongings in a U-Haul, and started toward Texas, and a lifestyle of secrecy.

TEN

FRIENDS IN LOW PLACES

ONE OF THE MARKS of God's watch care over his children in crisis is the arrival of his messengers of help at the moment we need them most. Mary Jo Ballentoni was the first of these messengers from God to come to our family in our time of need. Mary Jo was a student at Golden Gate Seminary during the time Scott attended there, and she and Lydia had become friends. Mary Jo was a drama major and performer who already had served a term in the Peace Corps in Columbia when she and Lydia met. She was a cheerful, entertaining, and willing volunteer.

She traveled from San Francisco to Colorado Springs to offer her help to Lydia and Scott as soon as the crisis struck. When she learned of the family's relocation plans, she never looked back; Mary Jo moved to Texas so she could assist the family. While Scott drove the U-Haul containing all the family's earthly possessions they could carry, Mary Jo drove their little Toyota all the way from Colorado to Texas, with Lydia, three-year-old Matthew, five-month-old Bryan with his portable oxygen tank, and stacks of clothing and other household items crammed into the tiny vehicle.

When the two weary women and children finally arrived at our home in Fort Worth, Mary Jo staggered into our house. She didn't say hello, she didn't explain who she was or what she was doing there, she simply groaned and said, "Don't say a word. Don't anyone say a word. I don't want to hear a word. Just point me to a bed and some peace and quiet!"

With those words, Mary Jo walked into our hearts. She lived with us during the early days of the secret; eventually she got her own apartment in Dallas. She remained in Texas for as long as Lydia and Scott needed her help. Her unselfish, Christlike spirit constantly inspired us all.

Once Scott arrived with the U-Haul, we began the job of getting the family settled at our home in Fort Worth. We had no idea how long they would be with us, so we unloaded all the boxes from the U-Haul, and then tried to find places to put them. Our townhouse —comfortable for Wanda and me—took on the appearance of a rummage sale, as we crammed in five more human beings, Scott and Lydia's belongings, Mary Jo's possessions, children's toys and clothes, and of course, Bryan's oxygen tank. Grateful as our house-guests were, we all recognized the need to start searching immediately for adequate housing.

Finding a suitable place for the family to live was not

easy. For one thing, Scott and Lydia were adamant that we could not move an AIDS family into a landlord's house without informing the owner. Because so much about AIDS was as yet unknown, they felt it only fair to give the landlord an opportunity to refuse to rent to us.

I began my search by calling realtors and homeowners who advertised isolated lake properties or farms in the newspapers. In my ignorance about the disease's possible contagion, I thought we might be required to maintain some distance between our family and our neighbors. Nowadays, we know that such misconceptions are nonsense, but at the time, we did not know any better. No suitable properties in our price range could be found.

Then, from seemingly out of the blue, a friend who was a real estate agent found us. Emily Nail and I had been classmates many years before. Her auburn hair made it inevitable that she be nicknamed "Rusty" Nail. A journalism major, Emily dreamed of being a writer. I had found her to be a great friend and encourager as we worked together planning worship services on our college campus.

For one of those services, I wrote an imaginary football game broadcast on radio station "WORD" from the "Stadium of Life." Emily recognized its potential, and insisted that I send "The Game of Life" to a Christian magazine. I did so, and the article was published. Another student at Baylor University, Jarrell McCracken, was a sports announcer. Jarrell asked permission to record the message and add crowd noises to it. "The Game of Life" recording sold three million copies and helped launch Word Records, of which Jarrell became president.

Emily went on to write articles and books of her own. Her writings focused upon helping people in crisis. She taught journalism for years, and became an expert in counseling women about coping with gender-related challenges.

By the time my family entered its crisis of the secret, my friend Rusty had become Emily Lunday and taught at a local university. She also had become a realtor. When I shared our secret with Emily, she offered to help.

Emily, Scott, and I met at a local restaurant to discuss our housing needs and the special type of real estate the secret made necessary. As we sat there, talking quietly while we ate, the waitress came up flustered and frustrated. She began to tell us what a bad day she was having. One of her kids had a fever and had to stay home from school. Her car hadn't started that morning. She was late to work. The other waitress didn't show up, so she was having to handle two stations. She just had to get some help!

When the waitress turned away, Scott deadpanned, "Boy, I'm glad I don't have her problems!"

As for Emily, she had no problem working on our behalf to secure housing for Scott and Lydia and the kids. She found a colleague at the university who owned a house he wanted to rent. Emily told him our secret, and he had no reservations about renting to us. In fact, he was glad to be of help. The house was perfect—big enough, in our price range, and best of all, within a mile of our townhouse.

We were selective in sharing our secret. Scott and Lydia's experiment with openness in telling their employers in Colorado Springs had not proven positive. Now that they were in Fort Worth and able to start afresh, a change in tack was agreed upon. Primarily out of concern for the children, we decided to keep the fact that the family had AIDS within our own circles, unless there was a specific reason someone else needed to know.

We recognized that there would be people who genuinely needed to know about the family's circumstances, as in our search for housing. No doubt, similar disclosure would be necessary as they searched for medical help, employment, educational opportunities, and social relationships.

Many times, however, silence was golden. Because of my position in public life, when people heard that our grandson Bryan was in the hospital, we knew we would receive cards, letters, get-well wishes, and phone calls.

We sincerely appreciated every expression of love and concern, but we quickly learned that not every question needed to be answered with a complete medical explanation and prognosis.

Often, people simply were being kind when they asked questions such as, "How is your grandson doing?" or "What seems to be the problem, anyhow?"

I have a constitutional commitment against lying. I simply will not do it. Lying goes against my Christian character and my personal integrity. Moreover, I soon discovered that I did not have to tell everything I knew about our family's situation to make it through most conversations. In answer to questions about Bryan's condition, as well as Matt's, I could honestly reply, "He has awful congestion in his chest," or "He has a problem with his blood," or "He is suffering from chronic diarrhea," or "He has a respiratory disorder, " or "His resistance is extremely low." All of these descriptions, of course, were symptoms of AIDS, but most people's curiosity was satisfied with a surface explanation. As such, we were able to maintain the secret without violating our personal principles.

We even managed to keep Bryan, Matt, and Lydia's hospital records secret. Since Bryan and Matthew were some of the first children with AIDS in the Dallas–Fort Worth metroplex, we wondered how they could be treated without becoming a part of public record. Fortunately, we discovered that many years before, prominent, "respectable" families, eager to hide the fact that their daughters were pregnant with illegitimate children, had encouraged the creation of a code to maintain confidentiality in the hospital. False names could be coded so hospital record keepers could recognize the true names and supply information for insurance claims and other purposes. But the public at large was unaware of the true identity of the hospitalized person. Nowadays, celebrities who are hospitalized often do something similar.

To protect the identities of our children, they became known around the hospital as Bryan and Matthew Green. No one picked up on the fact that a prominent religious leader had grandchildren in the hospital with AIDS.

When you have three out of four family members infected with a deadly disease, the major issue—after finding a place to live—is adequate medical help. Lydia was the point person in finding it. Not only a nurse but a victim and a mother of two sick children, Lydia was determined and persistent. During those first few months after finding out that she and her boys had AIDS, she was on the phone constantly, trying to find help. She called all over the nation in an attempt to discover what research was being done in the area of pediatric AIDS in general, and what specifically could be done for her children. The Centers for Disease Control in Atlanta, researchers in pediatric HIV in New Jersey and New York, a medical center in Houston, and dozens of other medical facilities became acquainted with the quiet, confronting voice of a plucky woman with a life-and-death cause.

In late 1985, Lydia probably knew more about pediatric AIDS research than any person in America, because seemingly she was the only person connected with the various groups working on the problem. For example, through her persistent telephone calls, she found a laboratory in New Jersey working on pediatric AIDS; she found another group in Long Island. Ironically, the two research labs were oblivious to each other.

Lydia told them, "Look, there's something immoral about you not talking to each other! I want a telephone conference call with you." She got the researchers from these two different groups, both of whom worked on pediatric AIDS issues, on the phone together in a conference call to talk about her needs and what her children were facing. That was the first time the researchers compared notes with each other.

Eventually, a national clearing house for AIDS Research evolved. But, at that time, although a great deal of research was being done on HIV, there was no coordinated effort, especially in the area of pediatric AIDS. Isolated groups kept popping up trying to solve the puzzle of this virus; many simply quit when they could not find a quick and inexpensive cure. Lydia, driven by a personal sense of urgency, called all these people, talked to them about her family's needs, and tried to find common denominators that might lead to answers for everyone.

Through Lydia's tireless efforts, she found several

medications that offered some hope, if not for a cure, at least for time. In late November 1985, during a conversation with a research physician in Houston, Lydia was told about a drug, Ribavirin, that seemed to help some AIDS patients.

Ribavirin originally was designed to help combat venereal disease. The same properties of the drug that helped thwart various strains of syphilis seemed to retard the spread of HIV. It could not cure the disease, but it slowed the ability of the virus to multiply. Unfortunately, Ribavirin had not been approved for use in the United States at that time. It was, however, legal and readily available in Mexico.

When Lydia continued to probe about the value of the drug, the doctor said, "I can't suggest that you do something illegal, but if I had a baby with AIDS, I'd be on my way to Mexico."

That's all Lydia needed to hear.

Two weeks later, I performed a marriage ceremony for the son of our friends Bill and Nadine "Pinky" Gray. The Grays had been missionaries in Mexico for more than twenty-five years before returning to the States. Bill now was coordinator of short-term international mission activities for Texas Baptists. Pinky— named for the bright color of her cheeks when she became embarrassed—was a Spanish-language counselor on my staff at the ACTS network. The best man at that wedding was a young Mexican medical doctor. His parents, also medical doctors, were at the wedding, too. They owned a clinic in Mexico City!

Bill and Pinky had returned to the States just in time. When we shared the secret with them, they offered to organize a Ribavirin smuggling operation. It was not long before we had a system for purchasing the medicine legally in Mexico, and bringing it into the United

States in the luggage of missions travelers, who regularly crossed the international border.

Whether the Ribavirin did any good is questionable. I am convinced that Ribavirin helped slow the debilitating effects of HIV during the early stages of Matt's disease. The real question, however, is what the border inspectors thought of all those religious people carrying so much personal medicine designed to cure venereal diseases!

Also as a result of Lydia's research, we discovered one of the most remarkable individuals who came to share our secret—Dr. Janet Squires. Janet became Bryan and Matt's pediatrician.

When we first met Janet, she treated infectious diseases at the Children's Hospital in Fort Worth. Her husband, Dr. Robert Squires, was a physician, too. Janet later became head of the Infectious Diseases Division at Children's Medical Hospital in Dallas when Robert accepted a teaching position at the medical school there. Janet became not only our physician but our friend.

Janet Squires was not afraid of AIDS. She had studied the disease since it first appeared, and although she was baffled about many aspects of HIV, she concluded that much of the public information concerning its transmission was little more than myths. Early on in her study of the disease, she realized that its primary means of transmission was through sexual contact with an infected person or by using intravenous drug needles contaminated by an HIV-infected person.

Janet acknowledged the obvious—that people such as Lydia and the boys had been infected through HIV-tainted blood—but emphasized that the number of people who contracted HIV in such ways was amazingly small compared to the number of people who carried the virus. More importantly, Janet taught us that by taking a few basic precautions we had nothing to fear from day-to-day normal contact with our victims of AIDS, or any others.

The Squireses have three children, one near Matthew's age. Janet and Robert were convinced that it was safe to be around AIDS patients, so they provided their own children as playmates for Matthew, and helped bridge the gap for his anxious parents (and grandparents), who tried to keep things as normal as possible in three-year-old Matt's disrupted world.

A devout Roman Catholic Christian, Janet lived out her faith daily by her service in Christ's name. She understood and honored our desire for secrecy, but lamented our need for it.

Now that the immediate needs of housing and medical attention were taken care of, we next focused on finding Scott a job. Quite naturally, we thought first in terms of ministry opportunities. As a promising pastor, with two academic degrees in religion and several years of pastoral experience, Scott would be an asset to the religious community. But what congregation would call a minister whose whole family had AIDS? Scott put his pastoral aspirations on hold.

Nevertheless, it was not long before we found an outlet for the gifts of compassion and concern that God had given him. Looking back, it is now easy to see how Scott's employment provision was part of God's providential plan.

Five years before our secret, when I served as the elected national leader of our denomination, I was challenged to create new strategies for a worldwide thrust of missions, as we looked toward the new millennium. One of my concerns, however, was that programs run by church bureaucracies often became so inbred and tradition-bound that new ideas and new energies easily evaporated. I increasingly became convinced that lay members of the church rather than "religious professionals" were best suited to impact the world, especially when it came to social problems.

Taking cues from the Peace Corps and from the Mormon missionary two-year strategies, I designed the Mission Service Corps. The idea was that people would volunteer for one or two years of service. Their skills would be invested anywhere in the world where they were needed. They could finance themselves or receive financing from partners in Mission Service Corps ministries.

Rather than falling victim to the slow, ponderous budgeting and committee processes of our denomination, the Mission Service Corps could be independent, flexible, and most of all, available. The idea captured the imagination of many lay people within our denomination. Today, thousands of people serve God and people around the world through the MSC. But I had no idea when I developed the Mission Service Corps that it would one day be the mechanism to support our family, as well as our secret.

The Christian social concerns unit in the Texas convention of Southern Baptists is called the Christian Life Commission. It is their task to deal with the difficult moral and ethical issues of our time. For eight years, I served as the chief executive officer of that organization. It seemed like a natural place to start in our search for a support ministry in which Scott could be employed. Besides, the current chief executive of the Christian Life Commission was Phil Strickland, one of my most beloved Christian brothers.

As I shared our secret with Phil, he suggested that Scott become a Mission Service Corps volunteer, charged with the responsibility of AIDS education for our denomination. Phil came up with the idea of an AIDS Task Force, a group of staff members who could research and dispense information to churches. He said, "As a church, we have needed to do something about AIDS. We've known that. We just haven't had any way to do it. If we can find Mission Service Corps support for Scott, then he could help us devise a way."

Phil's enthusiasm was encouraging, but Scott and I felt that before we could proceed, the people to whom the Mission Service Corps is accountable needed to know about the secret. The idea could never enjoy the blessing of God nor could we live with ourselves if we withheld any relevant information or fostered any deception.

The Home Mission Board in Atlanta is the governing structure for approving Mission Service Corps projects and personnel. Bill Tanner was head of that board at that time. Bill would have to be told the secret. So would Bill Pinson, the leader of the Texas convention. We arranged meetings and Scott or I sat down with them and told them the whole story. Both Bill Tanner and Bill Pinson responded in gracious, loving, Christian concern.

Within three months of Scott's departure from the church in Colorado Springs, we found enough people concerned about AIDS education and willing to back the new program financially that Scott was able to go back to work. The position gave Scott a purpose about which he could be passionate, a fellowship of understanding fellow workers, a salary, and a fringe benefit we have learned never to take for granted—health insurance.

Scott and Lydia had been covered under the insurance program of the Southern Baptist Convention as long as he was affiliated with our denomination. When he served in the Disciples Church in Colorado, Scott switched their insurance coverage to Lydia's policy through the hospital where she worked. When Lydia left their employment, she lost that policy. Consequently, when they moved back to Texas, they were insured under the grace period their previous policy provided, which was a few months of coverage intended to cover customers as they moved from one insurance coverage to another. When that coverage ran out, Scott and three sick family members who needed regular medical attention would have no private health insurance.

Before coming back into the Baptist system, Scott and I again felt that we had to share the secret with the person who needed to know. Darold Morgan is one of my closest friends and was head of the agency that had oversight of our denominational insurance program. Scott and I told him the whole story. We felt that Darold needed to know that we were talking about AIDS, especially in light of the costs that might be incurred in caring for three dying members of our family. Darold listened carefully and promised to do whatever he could to get the family back into our insurance program, but the final decision was up to the company. When Darold reported to us that Scott and the family had been accepted for insurance coverage, we considered it a huge answer to prayer.

Scott poured himself into his work. He served the Southern Baptists for the next two-and-a-half years, educating churches and pastors about AIDS and AIDS prevention. Soon he organized the AIDS Interfaith Task Force in Dallas, a group that raised awareness and provided education about AIDS not just for Southern Baptist churches but for anyone who would listen.

Scott became deeply involved in AIDS public policy issues. He was good at expressing the need for education and understanding. And at a time when many people had the misconception that AIDS was exclusively a homosexual disease, Scott knew firsthand that the public could not afford to make that mistake. Without exposing the secret, Phil Strickland suggested to the lieutenant governor of Texas, Bill Hobby, that Scott would be an excellent appointment to the Texas Study Commission on AIDS. Hobby took Phil's suggestion, and Scott served with creativity and distinction. A few years later, the National AIDS Commission was formed. In addition to Cabinet members and congressional members involved, the White House was to name a member from the general public, and Congress was to name two, one by the House, the other by the Senate.

Jim Wright of Texas was Speaker of the House at the time. A Presbyterian lay minister, Jim had worked with me on numerous projects through the years. The mistakes of judgment that led to his resignation from office have obscured the tremendous service to people that characterized his public life. Moreover, I counted Jim as a friend.

I arranged to meet him when he came to Fort Worth, and told him about what had happened to our family. Jim was profoundly moved. He knew of Scott's service in Texas, so without sharing the secret, he appointed Scott to the National AIDS Commission, despite pressures from other candidates who wanted the job. Scott chaired a subcommittee and served as the only clergy-person in the group. No one knew that

Scott had two family members who would die of the disease before the commission had completed its work.

We had much for which to be thankful during the Thanksgiving and Christmas holiday season of 1986. The family was comfortably relocated to Fort Worth. We had found excellent, informed medical help. And Scott was gainfully employed, doing something that would help his own family as he helped others.

We celebrated Christmas at Scott and Lydia's home. Luke and Joyce came from San Antonio, and Lydia went all out to make it a special time. She decorated the house and a Christmas tree, wrapped presents, hung stockings stuffed with small gifts and candy, the works! We sang Christmas carols, I read the Christmas story from the Bible, and we did all the other traditional things that are part of our family rituals. Someone peering in through the window never would have guessed that three people in the room had AIDS. Yet in the back of everyone's mind lurked the knowledge that this might be the last Christmas we would all celebrate together.

As it turned out, by the next Christmas, one of us was gone.

ELEVEN

THE UNTOUCHABLE BABY

AFTER CHRISTMAS, Bryan's condition went downhill rapidly. Wanda and I tried to help Lydia and Scott as they cared for him, although I often felt clumsy and helpless when it came to meeting the little fellow's many needs.

Once while I was visiting the family, Lydia needed to adjust Bryan's oxygen unit, so she unhooked the machine, took the tubes away from Bryan's face and handed him to me. I stepped into another room with him and sat in a rocking chair. I held Bryan's small, frail, fragile body in front of me, with my hand carefully cupped behind his head. As I talked to him, Bryan watched me. In that moment we connected. I was overwhelmed with an incredible love for this precious little boy.

I longed to tell him that all of life was not like the existence he endured through no fault of his own. I wanted to tell him that there are such things as pain-free days, and reasons to laugh, games to play, and trees to climb.

Bryan continued to watch me silently, quizzically looking at me as though to say, "Granddad, can't you help me?"

I cooed and hummed some more. Cooing and humming, even lovingly done, did not take away Bryan's pain.

When Lydia completed her chore, I said a hasty good-bye and left the house. As I drove away clutching the steering wheel of the car with all my might, I no longer could contain the anger and hurt I had been carrying in my soul. I pulled over to the curb, unable to drive, and simply lay my head on the steering wheel and wept.

I thought of Jesus standing at the tomb of his friend Lazarus, and I wondered if the anger Christ felt then was anything like the anger I now felt. I felt both angry and sad—angry at a world in which sin's separation from the intention of God is so often revealed in the struggling and dying of the innocent; sad because Bryan was dying and there was nothing I could do about it. If I ever felt the separation of the world from God—no, the separation of my world from God—it was now. My grief surfaced like a geyser gushing from deep within me. I wept and wept.

Not long after that, Bryan's little body could no longer stand the pain. When his lungs would not accept the oxygen from the respirator, he breathed his last. He died on February 2, 1986, less than nine months after he was born. His suffering was over, but the pain his death brought to Scott and Lydia continued. Their grief was exacerbated by the fear and ignorance of friends who found out only at Bryan's death the real cause of the infant's perpetual sickness.

One of the most disappointing reactions came from one of our pastoral friends. When he heard that Bryan had passed away, the pastor came to visit our family to offer his condolences. I was not home at the time, so he stayed and spoke briefly with Wanda.

In the course of their conversation, the pastor politely asked, "What was the matter with the baby?"

"He had AIDS," Wanda answered matter-of-factly.

The pastor stood to his feet, and almost as a reflex action, his hands flew up in the air as if he were trying to stop traffic. "Oh, oh, oh!" he said, as he backed away. The pastor quickly concluded his visit, and left our home without even shaking Wanda's hand. To his credit, the pastor drove from the Dallas–Fort Worth area all the way to Brownwood, Texas, to attend Bryan's small graveside funeral in Lydia's hometown. Nevertheless, it did not escape us that the first pastor who had an opportunity to minister to our family as victims of AIDS failed to reach past his fear. With some members of my family, he never got another chance.

The pastor was not the only person close to us who was afraid to touch someone with AIDS, or even the relative of someone with AIDS. The mortician who assisted in Bryan's burial was a family friend, but he was afraid to handle the tiny body. Consequently, under the mortician's supervision, Scott and Lydia themselves prepared Bryan's body for burial. They dressed their dead son in a sailor suit and laid him out in his hospital room. Their actions reminded me of the old days, when most people could not afford the services of a mortician, even if they had access to one. Families back then cared for their own in life and death.

Personally, poignantly, even sacredly, Scott and Lydia prepared Bryan's body for burial. They coped with the pain and handled the emotional hurt without breaking down until the very last. Then their grief overwhelmed them. But there was little time for tears; more hurt was yet to come.

When Bryan's body was placed in the casket to be transported to Brownwood, his head moved slightly, slipping into an awkward position. The mortician reached out to straighten the child's head, then suddenly recoiled in fear. He stepped back, pulling his hand back, as if he were about to touch a stove and suddenly realized it was hot.

"Would you mind straightening the baby's head?" he asked Scott and Lydia.

It was almost more than the couple could take. Nevertheless, they lovingly straightened Bryan's head and closed the casket. That moment cut like a knife into Scott and Lydia's hearts. It brought the truth into sharp, unmistakable focus—Bryan left this world as an untouchable.

Neither the pastor nor the mortician meant any harm by their actions. Nor could we blame them. The attitude about AIDS in 1986 was stark terror. People were afraid of catching AIDS from water fountains, from toilet seats, and even from casual kissing. With the news that the disease could be transmitted through the blood, many people assumed that mosquitoes could be agents of death, carrying the virus from person to person, much like malaria. None of these things were true, but truth had been taken hostage by fear. The pastor's and the mortician's fears merely reflected attitudes of most of our society at the time. Regardless, these calloused, insensitive actions hurt.

Lydia and Scott were not about to allow Bryan to be forgotten. They remembered and celebrated Bryan's life any way they could. They planted a tree as a memorial to Bryan. At Christmas each year, they hung Bryan's Christmas stocking next to Matt's. To help Matt comprehend and express his grief over the loss of Bryan, Lydia wrote a children's book entitled *I Miss My Baby Brother* (privately published).

After Bryan's death, Scott continued his work with the Christian Life Commission and the Mission Service Corps in Dallas. He organized churches in the area to help AIDS victims. He secured financial assistance for AIDS sufferers. He listened and counseled with AIDS victims as a pastor. And he preached at many of their funerals.

Sometimes he brought home babies whose mothers were HIV-positive or children who had the virus themselves. He and Lydia cared for those children as their own. Soon it became apparent to Lydia and Scott that part of the untold devastation of AIDS was that many of these little babies would be orphans because their parents had the disease. Others were infected themselves and needed someone to care for them, to help them die with as much dignity as possible. Many of their mothers lacked the energy to care for them, either because of their own debilitating disease or because of the constant drain upon them emotionally, economically, physically, and spiritually as they cared for someone with AIDS.

Lydia met with Stephanie Held, director of pastoral services at Temple Emmanu-El in Dallas, to discuss creating a pediatric day-care center for AIDS children.

No such center yet existed in the country, although Lydia had found a group of people hoping to start a center in New Jersey. Lydia gleaned a great deal of information and encouragement from the work the east coast group had done. She and Stephanie decided it could be done in Dallas.

They designed a center where children could stay a single day or the rest of their lives if necessary. They envisioned the facility as part care center, part hospice, and part nursing center. They established a board of directors, secured a grant of money from the Meadows Foundation, and purchased a small house in Dallas.

When the board met to choose a name for the center, they decided to name it for the first baby to die of AIDS in the Dallas area. With a bit of research, they discovered that this dubious distinction belonged to a little boy named Bryan. Lydia did not reveal that the Bryan they honored was her own son. Nor did she let on that she, too, carried the virus in her body.

The center became known simply as BRYAN'S HOUSE. Today, BRYAN'S HOUSE remains a part of his legacy, as the staff now serves as many as eighty children each week.

Lydia's obsession with keeping the secret that we were an AIDS family was not to avoid embarrassment or ridicule. It was to protect Matt and to provide as best we could a normal life for him as long as we had the privilege of enjoying him. Persecution of AIDS victims was real. After all, the media continued to chronicle cases in which HIV kids were thrown out of schools, jeered at, and even received death threats.

Ironically, the worst rejection Matt experienced as an AIDS victim was not from vicious kids at school or on the street. It was from Christian pastors and churches where we tried to enroll Matt in Sunday school.

TWELVE

THE CHURCH LETS US DOWN

IT ALWAYS HURTS when friends disappoint you; the hurt and disillusionment sear even more deeply into your heart when members of your own family turn their backs on you. To me, that's what our church is—family, the family of faith. I never expected that the church I loved so much would become our greatest source of pain.

Our sorrow began when Scott, Lydia, and I began searching for a church in which Matthew was welcome to attend Sunday school. Church after church turned us away. Good churches. Great churches. Wonderful people. Churches pastored by fine men of God, many of whom I had mentored. Nobody had room for a little boy with AIDS.

One of the first pastors to whom I broached the subject was a friend who led a large, affluent church in the Dallas–Fort Worth area. I asked him to come by my office. When he came, we exchanged pleasantries and I invited him to sit down.

"I want to show you something," I said.

I had a videotape of Dr. Janet Squires's children and Matthew playing in the park, along with Lydia and Janet. When I put the tape on, the television screen was filled with laughing, happy children. There was Matthew having a great time, laughing and running like the wind with the Squires's children. Matt was the picture of childhood happiness. Wearing a Superman cape, he ran to the camera, showed off his muscles, and said, "Somebody is in twuble."

I pointed out Matt to my friend as I said, "Now, I want you to know that this little four-year-old boy is my grandchild, Matthew, and you know that he and his family have just moved here."

The pastor nodded approvingly.

"And Matthew has AIDS."

My friend was stunned. His mouth fell open in surprise.

Rather than waiting for him to respond, I continued, "And I'm looking for a church that will let him come to Sunday school."

The pastor gulped hard.

I went on, "One of the women in the video is Lydia, my daughter-in-law. The other woman is Dr. Janet Squires, Matt's pediatrician. Janet is in charge of Matt's treatment. The children playing with Matt in this video belong to Janet and her husband, Robert, who is also a medical doctor."

I wanted to drive home the point to my pastor friend that here was a woman who knew as much about AIDS as any person alive. Her three kids and this AIDS child all played in the park together, running, laughing, doing all the usual kid things. And the doctor was not hesitant about it at all, because she knew her children were in no danger. Having made the point as emphatically as I could, I honed in on the purpose for our meeting. Looking the man directly in the eyes, I asked, "Would you think about whether you can get your Sunday school workers to give this child a chance to come to Sunday school?" I paused long enough for my words to sink in. Then I outlined a plan that I felt a church could implement in ministering to Matt and the other AIDS children who surely would soon be populating our Sunday schools: "My son Scott and his wife, Lydia, are willing to be in the classroom, either as teachers or teacher's assistants. I think if I were doing it, I would form a special unit on my Sunday school staff made up of people committed enough to ministry that they would be willing to have this child and others like him in their classroom. The parents of the other children in the class would have to be informed. We could have Dr. Squires speak to your teachers and to the parents of the children, to answer any questions they may have and to review some basic hygiene principles and inform the teachers of some simple precautions they should take.

When I felt that I had given the pastor a vision for how the program could happen, I stopped and gently asked him, "Can you do that at your church?"

The pastor was a tenderhearted man, and I thought I detected a tear in his eye as he glanced down at the floor and then back up at me. "I can try," he answered softly.

And he did try.

But he encountered strong resistance from the parents and teachers in the church. They were afraid to allow an AIDS child into their Sunday school. One medical doctor who attended that church added his voice to the concerns, "We don't know enough about this disease yet to tell you that it is safe to have the boy in the classroom with the other children."

I didn't hear from my friend for quite a while after that meeting. Had Matt not been my grandchild, had he belonged to some other family, I would have followed up more aggressively on my conversation with the pastor. But because of my relationship to Matt, and because of my past leadership positions in our denomination, I did not feel comfortable applying pressure to the pastor about admitting Matt to his Sunday school. I recognized that if the pastor took on this issue, it would create a crisis for him. He needed to know that, and needed to count the cost and decide it was worth doing, without any pressure from me.

Several months later, the pastor and I were talking about another subject when he suddenly said, "You know, I tried."

"Tried what?" I asked.

"I talked to the parents," he continued sadly. "It just didn't work."

I could tell by the look on his face that his church had refused to allow Matt to attend Sunday school there. "I thank you for trying," I replied, with what by this time was becoming an understanding of the deep-seated fear that motivated such decisions.

While I was waiting to hear from my initial pastoral contact, I invited another pastor to lunch one day, and laid out the situation to him in much the same way as I had to the first pastor.

He replied thoughtfully, "We need to do something

about this. I'll put it before my staff and we'll see how we can respond to it."

True to his word, he did put it before his staff. They held meetings in which the issues were thoroughly discussed. And they said no.

Being rejected by the church was bad enough, but their rationale saddened me beyond description. They were afraid that by accepting an AIDS child, they would scare off other prospects to their church. They were certain that once the word got out that they were "an AIDS church," nobody would come.

Scott and Lydia became more frustrated and disappointed that they could not find a church within our own denomination where they could worship and receive spiritual nurturing for Matt. Once I asked Scott and Lydia, "What if we could find a church but it was a long distance away?"

Lydia and Scott replied almost simultaneously, "We'll go anywhere!"

"We'll go to any kind of Christian church," said Scott. "It doesn't have to be a Baptist church . . . "

Lydia joined in, "We just want to have our child spiritually nurtured. Wherever the church is, whatever we have to do, we'll do it."

Scott began to explore possibilities for Matt outside our own denomination. He went to see a pastor he respected in the Disciples Church. When Scott told the pastor that Matt had AIDS, the pastor was willing to help.

"Bring him on," the pastor said. "We just won't tell anybody."

"No, I can't do that," Scott replied. "I can't place children in the Sunday school at risk of exposure to the virus without their parents' knowledge. It's not ethical. We have to be candid about Matt being there."

"Mmm," the pastor said as he mulled over the possibilities. He knew he never could get such a proposal through his church governing board, yet he wanted to help the family in some way. "Well, we could videotape the Sunday school classes and you could play them for Matt at home," he offered.

Scott answered, "Thank you, but that is not what our child needs. We can teach him Sunday school lessons at home ourselves. That's not the point. He needs to be with other children in a Christian learning environment. Showing him a videotape of other children in class or at play when he is not allowed to join them would be cruel."

The pastor agreed wholeheartedly, but had no other alternatives. Scott continued his search.

Carrying the secret was hard enough, but the rejection of the churches when we reached out for help was one of the most devastating aspects of our entire ordeal with AIDS. Especially for me.

When the church in Colorado let Scott go when his family had contracted AIDS, I felt the pain of disappointment. At the time, I believed that this response was an exception to the rule. I thought it was a case of a pastor lacking the courage to challenge his congregation to be creatively Christian. I considered it regrettable, even tragic, but I thought it was rare.

I believed in the potential of the church. The church always had been a part of my life. My early days of living in a house/church, mopping the floor of my bedroom after every baptismal service, were part of the warp and woof of my life. I had seen firsthand the change of attitude that came to people after their encounters with God. I had seen earnest, stumbling people respond to God and change their whole way of life.

I was convinced that while denominations and religious bureaucracies may stray as they jockey for power, groups of believers bound together under the Lordship of Jesus Christ were promised his presence and power to be Christlike. I believed that, in general, Christians were sensitive to Christ's commands. Given the right information, they would do the right things.

I was convinced, too, that Christians are some of the most compassionate people in the world. The root meaning of the word compassion is "a willingness to feel with or suffer with" another person or group. I repeatedly saw living evidence that the springs of compassion run deeply in the Christian's experience.

That belief was reinforced by my experiences in the churches I had served. In San Antonio, for example, I saw a massive congregation of nine thousand members willing to suffer with the poor and the hungry who had grown up around our downtown church. As soon as the members of that church understood the biblical mandate to minister to the lost, lowest, and least of society as well as the affluent and sophisticated, the congregation opened their hearts and connected with the hurting people around them.

Soon, barefoot, longhaired young people who wandered the streets of downtown San Antonio made their way into the large church. Many of those young men and women made decisions to follow Jesus Christ in the midst of that warm, loving, sophisticated congregation.

We didn't have to work hard to find people to whom we could minister. Multitudes of homeless, helpless people found us once word got out that they were welcome in our church. I still remember the voice of one of those untouchables as I took him in my automobile to find help for his specific need.

"They told me this was a good place . . . they told me this was a good place," he muttered over and over.

The compassion of God's people continued to be expressed at San Antonio First Baptist Church despite the anxiety of a minority who wondered aloud, "What are THEY doing in OUR church?" What *they* were doing was becoming a part of us—the family of God. At the end of the Sunday morning worship service, prostitutes and drug abusers, as well as the poor and the rich, joined hands and sang, "Lord, make Thy people one. Finish, oh finish, the work begun."

As one church after another rejected Matt, I wished I was back pastoring in San Antonio. I believed the church in San Antonio would accept an AIDS child without blinking an eye. The people there already ministered to people with every imaginable kind of need. During the twelve years that I served that congregation, never was there a group of people deemed untouchable, unreachable, or too difficult to deal with. That congregation had a spirit of compassion that came right from the heart of God.

My experience with that congregation and the knowledge of what God could do in and through a group of people who dared to reach out to the hurting world around them made me even more exasperated over the lack of acceptance for Matt. Although Matthew was one of the first AIDS children to knock on the church's door, he would not be the last. Certainly, our family's immediate concern was for Matt, but as I looked at the overall attitude of our church, I realized that they did not simply reject my grandson. They rejected the compassion that God wanted to express through them to broken, hurting people. Our churches were missing the opportunity of a lifetime.

I was not an impractical idealist. I knew Scott's family would represent a challenge to the church. I knew the power of fear. I thought, however, that challenge would be met and overcome. Scripture promises that perfect love casts out fear (1 John 4:18). That's one of the main reasons Jesus came to earth, lived, died, and rose from the grave. He came to defeat fear. Yet, in a strange and painful reversal of that promise, fear cast out perfect love when it came time for the church to minister to my grandchildren.

After a while, my friends in ministry avoided the subject of Matt's attendance at Sunday school, and I was reluctant to press them. In our silence, we all knew that the church was failing us. Despite our publicly announced intentions to follow Jesus—to live as he did— most churches were following the dictates of fear. Jesus voluntarily touched lepers, but he did not die of leprosy. He died at the hands of religious leaders who were so anxious to hold onto their power they wouldn't touch a leper to save their lives.

It hit me hard when I realized that the church as an institution had so failed that it could not summon the cleansing touch of Jesus for a four-year-old child. I vividly saw a reality I did not want to see. I saw that in many churches the strategy of gathering new members has become a science. We have learned well the techniques of church growth. To thrive in the user-friendly, what's-good-for-me era of modern Christianity, churches are supposed to be homogeneous, well-cared-for, comfortable, and entertaining.

The competition for new members is severe. The debt on buildings required for modern-day megachurches is high. We don't minister to those in need because we cannot afford to offend and lose paying members or prospects for membership. The fear of a deadly disease is enough to cause widespread panic in our church, not because the hurting people would fail to find us or refuse to come in, but because the comfortable and complacent people would be in such a hurry to get out.

All of my adult life, I have described the church as a family of faith. But living with the secret of AIDS taught me that just as many modern-day families are dysfunctional, so are many modern-day church families. The design of the family is right. The desire is present. But the doing of it has gone tragically awry. Often the root of the problem is ignorance and fear, instead of faith and love.

I was about to have my faith and love tested once again.

THIRTEEN

SKIP, TOO

"Dad, I'm gay."

Those words are some of the hardest a father can ever hear. About the only thing tougher to take is the addendum, "I am HIV-positive." When I heard both statements from my middle son, Skip, as Wanda said, "It almost did us in."

Skip told us the news about his HIV a few weeks after little Bryan died of AIDS. It was not the kind of message we wanted to hear after losing a loved one to the same disease.

Skip is one of the most talented and sensitive human beings I know. Handsome, spiritually inclined, musically gifted, with a high sense of humor, he always has had a lot going for himself. Like Scott, Skip struggled during his adolescence trying to find God's purpose for his life. Wanda and I lived through his rebellions and repentances; all the while, I was inwardly sure that he would end up serving God in his vocation. It was excruciating when it dawned on me that he was gay.

Not long after Skip graduated from high school, I began picking up clues concerning his sexuality. Occasionally, Mike and Scott would say things about Skip that caused me to wonder, but I passed off their remarks as typical male teasing. Still, I noticed that although Skip dated many young women, he never seemed comfortable in those relationships.

While Wanda and I lived in San Antonio, Skip moved to Houston. He became engaged to a young woman in our church with whom we were extremely pleased. They seriously contemplated marriage, when suddenly, they broke off their relationship.

I was surprised. Wanda and I loved Skip's fiancée and thought sure that Skip and the young woman would marry. Finally, the truth surfaced. Skip was homosexual. When he shared his sexual inclinations with the young woman, she walked away from the relationship.

Shortly after the demise of their marriage plans, Skip visited in our home in San Antonio. We talked about his feelings, and finally, I came straight out and asked him whether he was homosexual. It was not an easy question for me to ask.

Skip, however, didn't blink. He answered matter-of-factly, "Dad, I'm gay. God made me that way, and I can't do anything about it."

Skip's words hit me like a punch to the stomach by a heavyweight boxer. While I had sensed the signs of his homosexual inclinations, I had not confronted the issue in my own mind. Now, here it was, out on the table, challenging me, almost taunting me, to confront it in light of Skip's and my father-son relationship.

As one who takes the Bible seriously as the authority for life, there was no way I could justify homosexual behavior. Gently, but firmly, I reminded Skip of some of the Scripture passages regarding the subject. He was not convinced.

He answered by explaining to me that he perceived his homosexual inclinations to be genetic. He said, "If God made me this way, the Scriptures you are citing must be misinterpreted or misplaced."

We talked for a long time, and kept coming back to those same basic issues. When Skip left, neither of us had budged an inch in our positions about his homo-sexuality.

After Skip's departure, the reality of the situation ripped into my heart and mind with unremitting ven-geance. I felt instant, stomach-wrenching remorse.

One of the first reactions I had to the discovery that my son was homosexual was to ask myself, *What had I done as a father to make this happen? Good kids don't change their sexual preferences overnight, especially good kids who have been raised in a Christian home. Surely, I must have failed Skip somehow. His homosexuality must be my fault. But how?* I spent hours in anguished, in-tense self-examination of my flawed parenting patterns, searching for every little pitfall that might help explain what I considered to be my son's aberrant sexual pref-erences.

There had been no sexual abuse in our family. Nor had Skip grown up surrounded by warped concepts of human sexuality. None of the often cited reasons for homosexual tendencies—real or imagined—seemed to apply to Skip's and my relationship.

Time, of course, was the great enemy. *Did I spend enough time with this sensitive son?* "Quality time" was the argument I had bought when I knew my ministry robbed me of quantity of time with Skip and his brothers.

Now I realized I had blown it.

As I thought about the amount of time I had missed with Skip, I recalled with painful clarity a favorite family anecdote we had often told in humor. Once, when the boys were young, we had planned to enjoy a long weekend at the family's summer house on Lake Brownwood. As it often happened, I had a speaking engagement to fulfill, so I told Wanda to take the kids and go on to the lake ahead of me. I would come directly to the lake as soon as I was done.

Wanda loaded five-month-old Scott, three-year-old Skip, and five-year-old Mike into our old station wagon and hit the road. Along the way, Wanda stopped to get something to eat at our usual place, a truck-stop called *Jake and Dorothy's.* Wanda organized the troupe for their journey from the car to the cafe. She carried the baby. Mike carried the baby food. Skip dragged the diaper bag. As they entered the crowded restaurant, Skip complained at the top of his voice, "What this family needs is a *DADDY!*"

It was true. My family needed more time and attention than they received from me. Not that I had failed to make good use of my time with the boys. I had. I always remembered the special days, the birthdays when I took them to special places. I took each of them on an extended trip each year—just the two of us. It was disconcerting, however, to discover how much more those events meant to me than they did to the boys.

As I thought about Skip, I wallowed in my sorrow over missed opportunities and unfulfilled good intentions. I lacerated myself over misjudgments of discipline, praise, encouragement, and correction.

As a child, Skip had always done things differently than his brothers. The other boys enjoyed participating in active sports or attending sporting events as spectators. Not Skip. Even as a youngster, his tastes were different.

For instance, when he was only six years old, he and I dressed in formal attire and had dinner at La Tunisia, with its seven-foot-tall doorman and Arabian nights decor. For Skip's seventh birthday, we went to Ports O' Call, to enjoy its international cuisine and panoramic view from the top floor of a downtown skyscraper. Afterward, we attended the movie *My Fair Lady* at the Majestic Theater. The theater had an illuminated organ that came right out of the floor, with Miss Inez playing music before the movie began and during the intermission. Skip was enthralled!

Skip loved the stage; he was dramatic and gifted. I had driven myself nearly to exhaustion to be supportive of his aspirations of being on the stage. No matter how busy I was, his performances always took priority, because I knew Skip expected me to be in the audience.

As he grew older, Skip's life became more of a mystery to me. He came to religious activities more willingly than did his brothers—Skip was trying with all his might to please me. But behind all of that was a ghost that haunted him and eluded me.

For several years after Skip's and my initial conversation about his homosexuality, I beat myself up trying to figure out what I had done wrong, and if there was anything I could yet do to dissuade him from that lifestyle. Through much introspection, contemplation, and prayer, I finally found peace with my parenting. It came in two steps. The first was when I discovered the principle of limited liability. The second involved a principle I had often applied to other areas of my life, but not to Skip's sexuality—confession of sin.

Simply put, the principle of limited liability means that there are some things a parent cannot do. As parents, we can love, provide support, advise, and assist our children, but we cannot live their lives for them. They have to assume responsibility for themselves. It was a fact I knew, but a truth I had to discover.

I was greatly helped in this process by Alan Paton's poem, "Meditation for a Young Boy Confirmed." The insights of this writer spoke meaningfully to me. I have read his words scores of times, of which the following is an excerpt:

I see my son is wearing long trousers, I tremble
    at this;
I see he goes forward confidently,
    he does not know so fully his own gentleness.
Go forward, eager and reverent child,
    see here I begin to take my hands away from
    you,
I shall see you walk careless on the edges of the
    precipice, but if you wish you shall hear no
    word come out of me;
My whole soul will be sick with apprehension,
    but I shall not disobey you.
Life sees you coming, she sees you come with
    assurance towards her,
She lies in wait for you, she cannot but hurt
    you;

Go forward, go forward, I hold the bandages
   and ointments ready,
And if you would go elsewhere and lie alone
   with your wounds, why I shall not intrude
   upon you,
If you would seek the help of some other person, I shall not come forcing myself upon
   you.

If you should fall into sin, innocent one, that is
   the way of this pilgrimage;
Struggle against it, not for one fraction of a moment concede its dominion.
It will occasion you grief and sorrow, it will tor-
   ment you,
But hate not God, nor turn from him in shame
   or self-reproach;
He has seen many such, his compassion is as
   great as his Creation.
Be tempted and fall and return, return and be
   tempted and fall
A thousand times and a thousand, even to a
   thousand thousand.
For out of this tribulation there comes a peace,
   deep in the soul and surer than any dream,
And in the old and knowledgeable eyes there
   dwells, perhaps, some child's simplicity
That even asks for gifts and prays for sons.

As much as I wanted the best for Skip, I believed he
was settling for second best by giving reign to his homosexual urges. But I could not make him function as
a heterosexual. I believe God could help him discipline
his sexual drives, but Skip did not agree with me on
that.

The second aspect of making peace with my parenting was confessing my sin and my shortcomings. This involved confession and forgiveness on three levels. Since every sin is missing the mark of God's intention, sin is first and foremost against God. We sin against the intentions of the One who made us and loves us. God planned for our best good; we grieve him by failing to do or be what he intended.

Before we can find true freedom in any relationship, our sin against God has to be confessed—specifically named—and repented of—turned away from, not a slight change of direction, but a complete turning away from sin, a one-hundred-eighty-degree turnaround. Consequently, I took my parenting failures to the One I failed first, and asked God to forgive me for my failures as a parent, for improper attitudes, thoughts, words, and actions.

The second part of confession and forgiveness is tougher. The Bible makes it clear that we should also confess our failure to the ones we have failed. I went to my son Skip and asked his forgiveness for the times I had failed him. Assurances of forgiveness came in counseling sessions. Forgiving me did not deal with his inner anger, though. That anger emerged in bits and pieces over the years, and we dealt with it as it surfaced.

The third step was to forgive myself. I had to consciously choose to do so again and again, but it worked. The terrific burden was lifted. When accusations concerning my parenting of Skip came later, either from myself or from an external source, I honestly could say, "That is no longer on my back. It has been dealt with. I am forgiven, and I refuse to hold it against myself any longer than God held it against me. He says he has forgotten it, so I can forget it, too."

* * *

When Skip first tested positive for HIV, he went into the normal stages of inward denial and sorrow. He was living in Dallas and one night he called and asked if he could come to Fort Worth to see me. I welcomed him as always.

Our kitchen table had often been the place of family discussions, so when Skip arrived, we sat down at the table to talk. I nursed a cup of coffee as he poured out his heart. He paced the floor, then sat down for a few moments, and soon was back up pacing again, talking the entire time. He was trying to interpret the death sentence he recently received, his future, and his relationship with God.

Long before the news that he had AIDS, Skip overcame another personal problem—alcoholism. He had asked for God's help to change and he did it. When Skip discovered he was HIV-positive, he promised God some sober things about his behavior. But this was different. Changing his lifestyle would not make this crisis go away. He yearned for some of the lost opportunities of his life and talent. I joined him in lamenting lost opportunities of my own.

He'd sit for a while, then get up and pace our tiny kitchen. I listened prayerfully, trying to discern what God was doing in his life, and what—if anything—I could say or do to help.

After a while, I said, "The test of the experience, Skip, is always what it does to honor and glorify Jesus Christ, and what the Spirit of God does to implement change in our lives. What he is doing in your life will reveal itself. We must be patient."

"Patient!" he half-joked. "You and I are poor people to talk about patience. Neither of us has much of it."

Long into the night we talked and prayed and cried and hugged. As he got in his car to leave, I sat thinking of all the times across the years when we had come heart-to-heart, but not mind-to-mind.

Skip's and my differences of opinion are deep, but we love each other through them. I refuse to believe that same-sex expressions of sexuality are part of a valid, biblically Christian lifestyle. Whether a person is born with a predisposition toward homosexuality remains an issue for medical debate, but to me it is irrelevant. Regardless of our predispositions, I believe that whether a person is heterosexual or homosexual, sexual drives can and must be disciplined in their expression according to biblical principles.

Skip's definitions, his vocabulary and attitudes, his rejection of the authority of some of the Scriptures I hold dear are chasms between how he perceives God and how I perceive God. We continue to converse about God, but our communications are often flawed. Nevertheless, Skip and I have chosen to meet on the high ground of loving despite our differences.

We have slogged through swamps of estrangement of spirit. It has been fiercely painful for us both. Wanda joins in the pain, but as a mother she seems to manage it better than I do. Nevertheless, through conversations and counseling, she and Skip and I have sought to express our questions and frustrations. That whole process has been healthy, but not easy. We share a mutual respect and care, but the pain goes on.

When Skip first told me of his homosexuality, we talked a long time. I hugged him then and many times afterward. Later, I wrote him a letter outlining my love for him and my acceptance of him as a person regardless of his behavior. I expressed to him my belief that we are all born with "defective equipment" of some sort. The question is: what are we going to do with it? I told him that I believed he could rechannel his sexual drives into a positive, celibate lifestyle, and I encouraged him to do so. I emphasized that no matter what he did, I would always love him.

The fact is, however, Skip was unprepared to feel the hugs or receive my love. Through many a conversation, we covered the same ground. He could not hear me. He wanted agreement and approval. I could only give love and understanding.

After the HIV-positive diagnosis, we drew closer together once more. There was an awkward, tenuous truce between us despite our disagreements. In an interview on the ABC television network, Skip said of me, "I was asking for his acceptance. What the man had to offer me was his love."

Bryan was dead, Lydia and Matt were in failing health, and now, Skip was HIV-positive, with a low T-cell count, which means his T-lymphocytes, the cells that ordinarily fight off diseases, were being destroyed. Skip had AIDS.

He continued working and remained a productive part of his community. He has his own business, a frame shop and art gallery. He moves creatively and caringly among the dying, comforting and serving other victims of AIDS. How long he will live with AIDS is unpredictable, but he has a remarkable calmness about dying. In the meantime, he is making every day count.

He loves God. His faith is mystical and emotional. He responds more than he reasons about spiritual things, but he centers his faith in Jesus Christ. Granted, there are elements of my son's lifestyle that I do not understand and cannot condone. On the other hand, my son is much more than his sexuality. And I love my son.

Strange, isn't it? The entire picture of AIDS changes when you put the faces of your own family members in the frame. My friend, comedian Jerry Clower, told me a story that drove home this message to me. During the days of the national debates over amnesty for those who refused to participate in the Vietnam war, Jerry was on a Boston talk show. After a pleasant conversation, the host suddenly told the audience, "When we come back from this break, Jerry will tell us what he thinks of amnesty." Ninety seconds later, Jerry had to answer. His response was classic.

"Now, let's see," Jerry drawled. "Are we talking about your boy or my boy? If it's your boy, let's leave him in that foreign country where he ran. But if it's my boy, I'd just as soon he come home."

FOURTEEN

SCHOOL DAZE

By 1987, the AIDS in Matt's body began to manifest itself. The adults in his life probably noticed it more than he did; Matt did not notice anything different. After all, he had been sick all of his life, so there was nothing new about more trips to the doctors for checkups, and more trips to the hospital for shots. Still, he was a little boy who loved to run, play, laugh, and have a good time. As far as Matt was concerned, these were the best days of his life—and in many ways they were.

A take-charge kind of guy, at Disney World in Orlando he quickly became an expert on the location of everything. He was five years old. We have pictures of him sitting on a park bench with a map, pointing the way to his Disney-weary Granddad. Another picture captures him at one of the signpost maps pointing the direction to five adults who had lost their way.

When Matt was old enough for preschool, he was small for his years but eager to go to school. Scott and Lydia approached the Dallas public school system officials to find out their policy on AIDS children. To their dismay, they discovered there was no policy. Like many other school systems, Dallas had avoided the issue of AIDS rather than confront it.

Scott and Lydia informed the school system that they wanted to enroll an AIDS child, and suddenly "somebody else's problem" came knocking on Dallas's door. Fortunately, with Scott's access to information about AIDS through his work, and Lydia's help in searching out school policies in other locations, they were able to offer invaluable suggestions to the Dallas school officials as they composed a set of guidelines concerning the admission of AIDS children.

It was not a forgone conclusion that the Dallas school system would admit an AIDS child. Yet it is amazing to me how the Father works to put the right people in the right places to accomplish right things. At the time that Scott and Lydia wanted to enroll Matt, the president of the Dallas School Board was Mary Rutledge. A housewife and mother in the Oak Cliff area of Dallas, Mary also was a faithful Christian and a deacon in Cliff Temple Baptist Church. When she was made aware of Matt's condition, she approached the issue with tremendous energy and skill.

The Dallas public school superintendent was Linus Wright. He was about to be appointed assistant secretary of education for the U.S. Department of Education. An outstanding public educator, he had no desire to leave this unfinished task for public scrutiny as he departed for that national position. A study of the issues and necessary negotiations were quietly yet thoroughly completed. The Dallas school district policy of accepting HIV-positive students was adopted.

Matt was one of the first students admitted by the Dallas policy. The first year Matt was to go to a magnet school in downtown Dallas. The teacher and principal were briefed on the situation. The school nurse received instructions on how to handle any emergencies that might occur. When all the bases were covered, Matt was able to attend preschool.

My family will be eternally grateful to Mary Rutledge, Linus Wright, and their coworkers for their courageous leadership in making a five-year-old outsider an insider.

Educating the educators had to be done all over again the following year when Scott and Lydia enrolled Matt for his first year in regular school. The school he was to attend was in the neighborhood in which he lived, but some of the school administrators wanted to place Matt into special educational tracks, located at a distant school in Dallas. Scott and Lydia refused. It would not only be inconvenient but damaging to Matt to be carted off somewhere else to receive the school experience all the children in his neighborhood had nearby.

Putting Matt in school was not a passive experience for Scott and Lydia. They continually were involved, not simply in Matt's education, but in the education of school personnel concerning AIDS. They had conferences with principals, teachers, and parents all the way through Matt's school experiences. Information was needed and difficulties had to be spotted before they became insurmountable problems. For instance, they had to clarify the law about confidentiality to one principal who didn't seem to catch on to how sensitive the issues were that swirled around the subject of AIDS.

As Matt's school days began, again the right people were in the right places. God seemed to surround Matt with people who would show him the compassion and care that he was not able to find in the church. Lakewood Elementary School, a public school—Matt's school—exemplified far more of the Spirit of Christ than did many of the institutions that bear his name.

It wasn't that the people at Lakewood did not have their fears and reservations about a child with AIDS. But where there was fear, they overcame it. Where there was ignorance or confusion, they sought to provide the truth.

For instance, when Mrs. Marian Hammert, Matt's kindergarten teacher at Lakewood Elementary School, was told an AIDS child would be in her classroom, she knew so little about the subject that she had to have a special briefing. She was willing to teach Matt, but she first requested she be tested for HIV herself, so if she got infected later, she could prove that it was job-related! Such was the dread of the uninformed.

At the end of Matt's first year of school, however, Mrs. Hammert came to our family members and said, "I love Matt so much. If there is any problem next year, I am also qualified to teach first grade. I would be glad to shift grades to be his teacher." We were deeply moved by the transformation in her understanding of AIDS, but even more so by her willingness to care for Matt.

I spent a lot of time at Lakewood Elementary School. I dropped by to see Matt so frequently, the teachers and students must have thought I had returned for a refresher course! Actually, since I often was occupied on weekends, I made a special effort to stop by the school around noontime, so Matt and I could be together at lunch. He ordered special hamburgers and milkshakes, and I brought them with me to school. We joined the line of children to the lunchroom. Matt became the envy of several of his friends who were impressed with the gray-haired grandfather who came to school, bringing special lunches.

Besides getting to see Matt, the highlight of my midday visits was walking the playground during recess. Matt always made a special point of introducing me to his friends. Whenever I met children who regarded Matt not as a boy with AIDS but simply as a friend, I thanked God for Lakewood Elementary School and the love that was there.

It was not until several years later that I learned one of the keys to Lakewood's success. A group of Christian parents meet regularly to pray for Lakewood Elementary School, for its principal, the teachers and staff members, and the children who attended there, as well as their parents and siblings. Who says you can't take God into the public schools!

FIFTEEN

A SHOCK
TO OUR
SYSTEM

OUR FAMILY GREW accustomed to coping with AIDS on a daily basis, and we got to the place where we felt we knew what was coming and could prepare for it. Frankly, we knew Lydia's health was deteriorating rapidly and we grappled with the reality of another Allen funeral in the near future. But nothing could have prepared me for the sudden death of my best friend.

Luke Williams and I had known each other for over forty years. We had worked together for more than twenty years. He was like a brother to me, and when he died, a part of me died as well.

By 1991 Luke had become director of development for the Baptist Hospital in San Antonio. He had organized the San Antonio Baptist Hospital Foundation, and as president of that organization, he was in charge of health-care fund-raising for the nonprofit hospital.

From the moment Luke learned of Lydia's and the boys' infection with HIV, he never stopped praying that they would be healed. Even when it was certain that the family members had full-blown AIDS, Luke never gave up believing that God might yet heal them. In the meantime, he worked feverishly at finding medicines and treatments through which God might choose to bring relief to the children. In his methodical, administrative ways, he kept up with every test, and tracked every change in their T-cell counts. When there was any progress in the search for a cure of AIDS, or even a new medicine that might ease the pain of the disease's victims, Luke knew about it.

None of our family members were surprised when Luke discovered some people in San Antonio who were working on a possible cure for AIDS, or at least a treatment they thought could retard the virus' symptoms in some individuals. The bulk of the group's work took place in Mexico, so in the spring of 1991, Luke arranged for Lydia to spend three weeks in Mexico, while she received the treatments. Lydia did not see much progress, and she began to resign herself to the inevitable fact that her days on earth were dwindling.

The strain on Luke was enormous.

Luke and I stayed in touch by telephone every day, even though I was in Fort Worth and he was in San Antonio. We'd call each other to share reports about what was happening with the children, and to encourage and pray for each other's personal and family needs. The love we shared was like that of the Old Testament characters Jonathan and David—pure, unselfish, eternal.

*   *   *

Luke had not been in good health for a long time. While we were in San Antonio working together, Luke developed a viral infection that severely depleted the potassium in his body, causing him to be extremely sick. He never totally recovered from that illness, but by supplementing his daily potassium intake, he was able to function normally, other than a problem with strength and control in his left hand. Luke continually exercised that hand by squeezing a rubber ball he carried around with him most of the time. He played tennis, and kept physically active throughout his life. He maintained a regular regimen to keep his body in good shape.

Knowing Luke's physical disciplines, I was shocked to learn that he had suffered a massive stroke. I was in Fort Worth when I received the call; I flew to San Antonio on the first flight that would get me there.

When I arrived, Lydia and the other family members had gathered at the hospital. Lydia was in the emergency room talking to the doctors, finding out what was happening.

As soon as she came out, I could tell by the look on Lydia's face that Luke was not going to make it. Trying to remain calm, Lydia said to me, "He is going to die. I've seen the brain scans and it looks as though his brain has exploded. There's no possibility for him to live . . ."

Luke hung on through the night, but the next day, July 26, 1991, was his last. He was sixty-two years of age. Even though Luke never regained consciousness, I was glad I got there before he died. And although he may not have heard my words, I was thankful for the opportunity to tell Luke one more time how much he meant to me.

*   *   *

I am convinced that Luke Williams died of AIDS—not in the usual sense, but I believe that the stress the disease caused to Luke and Joyce and the other members of his family finally got to be more than his system could take. Luke was a warm-spirited, focused man. He kept his business private and had a hard time talking about personal things. Consequently, he bottled up a lot of his feelings, and kept them inside himself. The stress of watching Lydia's health going downhill, despite his best efforts to ease her pain and prolong her life, combined with the burden of the secret, became too heavy for him. AIDS killed him.

I was deeply disturbed by Luke's death, especially by the suddenness of it, but I was thankful that God delivered Luke from having to deal with the ordeal of his daughter's death. I preached Luke's funeral message to over one thousand people who came to pay their last respects to a godly man. Lydia took her daddy's death and funeral very hard, yet in her inimitable resourcefulness, she viewed the gathering of the relatives as an opportunity to begin saying her own good-byes.

She held a meeting of her dad's side of the family while they were in San Antonio at the time of Luke's death. Lydia used the occasion to bring the whole Williams family together to talk to them about her dying. Some of the family members had tried to avoid facing the facts of what she was going through. Lydia refused to allow them to maintain their illusions any longer.

She told them, "I'm going to die, and I'll be with Daddy before long. I just want you to know that. I want to die with dignity. I don't want to be dragged through it. I want you to know I'm going to die and I want to deal with this candidly with you."

The family members blinked back their tears as Lydia

talked freely about her going to be with the Lord. Everyone in the room recognized this as a turning point in Lydia's dealing with her pain. Prior to this point, she had been reluctant to say much about it. Lydia was convinced that to talk about pain was to increase it. She was very sensitive to pain in others—as a nurse, she had lived in its shadow constantly—but she rarely spoke of her own. For the past nine years, AIDS had silently attacked her body, slowly but surely sucking the life out of her. During that time, Lydia worked herself ragged, trying to speak for others who had the disease, yet maintaining a stoic silence about what the disease was doing to her own body. So successfully had Lydia masked her emotional and physical pain, many people did not know she was brutally sick. Now they did.

From that day on, Lydia went about getting ready to die. She recognized the debilitating effects of AIDS that ravaged her body, and she knew that it wasn't going to be long before the family gathered for another funeral. She wanted to leave no loose ends in her relationships, so she arranged to speak personally with every family member and friend she could contact. She wrote each of us letters of appreciation and farewell. Lydia prepared for her departure with the same thoroughness and single-mindedness that she did everything else. She went about it as methodically as her daddy would have, had he been given the chance.

She made a list of people she wanted to say good-bye to, and visited every one of them, or had them visit her to have a final, closing conversation. She visited with her sister, her brother, her brother-in-law, her friends, one after another, and toward the end, with Wanda, and with me.

* * *

I was preparing to leave for a trip to Thailand, on a matter relating to a college with which I am affiliated in that country. I was taking a group of about thirty people to visit the college and to tour parts of Thailand and Hong Kong, with an excursion into China. A few days before I was scheduled to depart, Lydia called me in Fort Worth and said, "I want you to come over. We need to have our conversation about my death."

Knowing full well what she was doing, the bluntness of her statement stunned me nonetheless. I said, "Well, okay, when did you want to do that?"

"As soon as possible," she replied.

I said, "I'll be right there."

I drove across town from Fort Worth to Dallas, my mind in a blur. *How do I prepare my heart and mind for this conversation?* I had helped many people face their own deaths. I had held people's hands at their bedsides in the hospital as they entered eternity. I had prayed with people that they might find peace with God before they met him face-to-face, but this was different. I could not recall a time when I had been asked to face death in such a perfunctory manner.

It wasn't easy. Besides being the end of the emotional roller-coaster ride Lydia had been on for nearly a decade, this was my daughter-in-law, my son's wife, the mother of my grandchild; this was Lydia, whom I loved.

By the time I arrived, Lydia had arranged to be alone. Scott knew what she was doing, so he and Matt had gone someplace else for the day. Lydia answered the door, and invited me into the living room. She was able to move around, but not without a great expenditure of energy. She shuffled alongside me as we made our way to the sofa. Although Lydia masked her pain better than anybody I've ever seen, it was obvious that

she was in intense physical agony. In the months prior
to this, she had lost a lot of weight, but now, because
of the medication she was receiving, her body had an
unusually puffy look.

We sat there on the sofa and for more than three
hours we talked quietly about our lives. We recalled
special memories that made us laugh. Other memories
brought tears to our eyes. More than a few times, my
words were muffled by the lump in my throat.

Lydia had written me a note to say thank you. In her
own handwriting, each word painstakingly written, the
note said, "You know what we thought about you by
the fact that, in the greatest crisis of our lives, you were
the one we turned to."

We talked frankly about the fact that she was dying.
She said, "I have one thing I worry about. I don't
want Matt to forget me, and I don't want him to be
angry because I'm leaving. I want you to help me with
Matt. Please let him know how much I love him."

Could there be an easier assignment? Matt and Lydia
were so irrevocably connected, it was obvious that their
love would continue to be strong. Besides, Lydia had
prepared videotapes of herself that Matt could watch
after she was gone. Both Matt and Lydia loved dolphins, so in one of the most memorable video clips she
had made only a few weeks prior to our conversation,
Lydia reminded her son one last time, "When you see
the dolphins, I want you to remember how much I
love you."

I said, "Lydia, there's no way Matt is going to forget
you. He looks like you and acts like you."

Still, Lydia was concerned that Matt might resent
her living arrangements their final year together. During that time, Lydia had moved out of the family
home. Because of the stress she experienced relating to

Scott as he dealt with the pressures of AIDS, Lydia felt that she needed more "space." None of us could discern how much of that attitude came from the internal effects of the virus itself, her ways of dealing with pain, or from the stress-induced deterioration of their marriage relationship. At that point, debates over cause and effect were irrelevant.

Nevertheless, it was jarring for all of us when she decided to move from their house to an apartment three blocks away. Since Lydia and I always had been close, she told me in advance that she was moving out.

I knew better than to argue with her, but I asked her, "Why do you have to do this?"

"I've just got to have space. I can't deal with this on a day-to-day basis. I've got to have some place to retreat to. I'm not leaving the country. I'm moving out, though."

Scott and I talked about Lydia's move, too. He was angry about it because it didn't make sense to him. It increased expenses. It was an adjustment for Matthew. It created more tension between him and Lydia; and for what?

Matthew, of course, got caught in the middle of his parents' emotional strain. Matt stayed overnight with Lydia on a regular basis, but he was angry that she had moved into the apartment and could not understand why their family was not living together. None of his adult family members could explain it to him, because we did not know the answer ourselves.

No doubt, part of the explanation lay in Lydia's inability to control the life of her family any longer. Lydia had always been a take-charge type of person. It was one of her stronger qualities, and in the early days of her marriage to Scott, the trait worked to their advantage. As long as Scott remained a grown-up adolescent, Lydia was in her element. She was taking care of her husband. As Scott became more mature, that threatened Lydia's turf, and created stress between them. The stress probably would not have been insurmountable had it not been exacerbated by AIDS. Although they were driven closer together because of their mutual pain, the constant dealing with disease, dying, and death took an awful emotional toll upon their lives.

Lydia lived in her own apartment for about five months. When she drew closer to her death and grew continually weaker, she realized she could no longer handle things alone. Scott went and got her, and moved Lydia back in to the family home.

Now, as we sat and visited, I assured her that as Matt was able to absorb the information, I would do my best to help him better understand the enormous stress the disease had placed upon their family.

Lydia and I also talked about some of the things she had learned about God in the road of suffering on which she traveled. We talked about the deep wounds Lydia had endured from people who called themselves Christians, yet had not acted Christlike. Lydia recognized that the attitudes and actions of those individuals had to be regarded as human failings. She forgave each one and carried no animosity with her to her grave. We also remembered the people who had come to our rescue, and thanked God for them.

We discussed the shock she felt a few months before this time, when her father and my friend, Luke, had died. Her dad's death brought us full circle to the reason I was sitting there.

I talked to Lydia about eternity, about her faith, and what she believed was going to happen when she died.

She looked me straight in the eyes and said, "You know, frankly, I don't know. When you get right down to it," Lydia said, "we humans don't know very much about death and what's beyond it. I see it as a great adventure. I am sure about reuniting with Daddy and Bryan. I don't know what form we are going to be in, but I know I'm going to be with them. Beyond that it's an adventure." There was no wavering in her voice.

I did not want to leave, but had been there a long time and I could tell Lydia was tiring. "Are you all right, Lydia?" I asked.

She smiled faintly, and yawned. It was almost as if she could read my thoughts. She said, "I didn't ask for this disease. I have done my best with it. I'm tired and it's wearing me out and I can't go much farther."

In our closing conversation, Lydia was as pragmatic as ever. I was concerned that my travel plans might take me away at a time when she needed me the most. I said, "Now, Lydia, I am scheduled to go to Thailand, and you are telling me you're going to die soon. Should I cancel this trip? I surely don't want to be gone when you die."

"No, I think you ought to go," she answered thoughtfully. "Airplanes fly both ways. If I die before you get back, somebody will get word to you."

I asked Lydia what she thought about her funeral. She said, "Let's do what's comforting to my mother."

I said, "Well, are you going to be buried in a church service?"

She replied quickly, "Oh, yes; let's do whatever is comforting. Whatever Mother needs. I'll be gone."

We made arrangements for Lydia's funeral to be held at Shiloh Baptist Church of Dallas, the church where Luke had first served, right out of seminary, as minister of education, and where Lydia had first worshiped as a child.

I left that day knowing that Lydia and I had knit our hearts together for the last time.

As I walk to the door, she simply said, "Thank you." I knew what she meant.

I told her that I loved her. She told me that she loved me. Those were our last words spoken to each other in our final conversation on earth.

I was in Thailand when the call came. Lydia was right —the plane flew both ways. I arrived back home the day before she died. I went immediately to Lydia and Scott's home in Dallas. By that time, the hospice people were on the scene, taking care of Lydia. I developed a deeper appreciation for the hospice movement as I observed their sensitive assistance, which allowed Lydia to die with dignity, the way she had desired . . . at home with her family.

At Lydia's funeral, no one mentioned AIDS. It was the last time we, as a family, gathered in church to protect the secret. As we sat in the Shiloh Baptist Church in Dallas, as Lydia's mother had requested, I was moved by sorrow and touched by the music and by the words spoken by Lydia's devoted friend, Mary Jo Ballentoni, and by Phil Strickland, our longtime friend who had helped arrange Scott's first job after he was let go by the church in Colorado.

During the ceremony, Scott and Matt were by my side. I could feel Scott's anger rising as he sat rigidly through the songs, eulogies, and prayers. After the service, Scott got up and left the church without a word to anyone. Before doing so, he said to me in a terse, quiet voice, "Nobody said the word AIDS in the whole service."

He was right. It was then that I saw how wrong we had been in trying to keep our secret, even if we had done it for the right, noble reason of trying to protect Matt. Almost everyone in the church knew that Lydia had died of AIDS. But no one said it.

Perhaps our silence, even in the face of Lydia's death, was partially because Lydia herself had been so adamant about keeping the secret. But that did not mean she was unaware of the awful, deafening sounds of silence. Although she never once spoke publicly of her inner turmoil, she articulated it well in an article, "Wearing the Scarlet Letter 'A'," published anonymously in the *Baptist Standard* in 1987. This was Lydia's rationale for carrying the burden of a secret:

When teaching phonics to my preschooler, we started at the beginning of the alphabet. "This is the letter 'A'," I said. "Do you know a word that begins with A?"

The poignant reply came, "A is for AIDS."

So it is in our lives: A is for AIDS. It is the beginning and ending of every facet of our existence. We are the new UNTOUCHABLES.

I had become infected with the AIDS virus by a blood transfusion while still pregnant with our first child. As a result, our baby also contracted the virus. Although I was frequently ill and fatigued, I passed it off as being the "new mother syndrome."

Our baby was quite ill as well, requiring weekly trips to the doctor, and I blamed much of my exhaustion on stress. Having no idea that I was car-

rying the AIDS virus, two years after the birth of
my first child, I became pregnant again.

Our second child was premature and also had
multiple medical problems. When the new baby
was five months old, I received a call from the
blood bank that had supplied the blood for my
transfusion. They said that the donor who had
given the blood for my transfusions had AIDS.

My world started reeling. As soon as I heard the
words, all of the events of the past three years
came into focus with a searing clarity. The children's inability to stay well; the doctor's frequent
head shaking and statements: "This is rare." "The
medicine should have worked."

Within two months, I had lost most of what
constituted my world. Our baby was in critical
condition with days or weeks to live. My husband
had lost his job and career when his employer
found out that his family had been touched with
AIDS. Our older child had to be removed from
day care. We were asked not to return to our
church. Our confidentiality had been breached
and as word spread throughout our community,
we quickly fled and relocated in another town. We
were too terrified to risk harassment and persecution.

Several months after our move, our baby died
and the second phase of my isolation began. This
isolation was self-imposed, by fear.

The few relationships I have had are superficial
and almost totally based on fabrication. How
could I truthfully answer simple questions: "Why
did you move here?" "What was wrong with your
baby?" I couldn't talk about the fact that my heart
was breaking every time I looked at my little boy.

I couldn't share the fact that my marriage was fragmenting from the incredible stress in our lives. I couldn't "act sick" lest someone get suspicious. So I hid my symptoms and pain.

I didn't dare reveal anything about the severity of my son's illness lest my child be totally ostracized from all socialization. I couldn't even contact former coworkers to explain why I had suddenly disappeared. I was in a new city with no friends, no church, no "home" (we had left "home"), no job, a struggling marriage, a very sick child, and a grief for our baby who had died. I had never been so alone in my life.

We reached out to a local church. The pastor was supportive but when he asked parents about the possibility of our child attending Sunday school, the parents said NO. We do not attend church now. The rejection runs too deep. To Christians, I would say that AIDS cripples not only the body but the heart. At a time when the AIDS victim is dealing with death and dying, heavy financial burden, and physical debilitation, they need support, care, and concern—not rejection. If there ever was a time to reach out and touch the "lepers" of our day, it is now.

I wear the SCARLET A. I keep it well hidden. You may never see me cry or realize from my appearance that I have been infected by the virus. Nevertheless, I have been shattered. I need love, compassion, and community to help me make it from day to day. I have done nothing immoral or illegal to contract this disease, but those who HAVE hurt just as deeply as I. Their needs are as great or greater than mine for a compassionate and loving response to AIDS.

Lydia carried the secret all the way to her grave.
Now our dear Lydia was gone. As was Bryan. Matt's
health was starting to fail, as well.

Scott and I decided it was time to tell our secret to
the world.

SIXTEEN

GOING PUBLIC

BECAUSE OF MY LEADERSHIP POSITION in one of the largest branches of the Christian church and my work in the area of communication, I was fair game for any reporter who wanted to break the story that four members of my family had AIDS. In fact, we were haunted by the specter that all of our efforts to keep the story secret would be to no avail. A story as sensational as our is tough to keep quiet.

There were several times reporters discovered our secret and nearly exposed it. That kept us feeling paranoid about our privacy. When Scott and I learned of reporters who were on to us, we went directly to them to plead our case. We told them about Matt, a little boy whose life could be marred by having to deal with the pressure public exposure would bring, and all were willing to hold the story—temporarily.

When Bryan died, his cause of death was listed as respiratory failure. Collectively, we held our breath as we wondered whether the first AIDS-related death of a baby in the Dallas–Fort Worth area would draw media attention and exposure.

It didn't.

We frequently accuse the news media of insensitivity and thoughtlessness in their pursuit of sensational stories. Certainly some of the press deserve such accusations. For the most part, however, we found the media fair, kind, and considerate in its handling of our experience with AIDS. Most reporters who discovered our story were willing to delay publishing the details for Matt's sake. As long as we assured them that they could be the first with the story in their particular medium—when we chose to disclose it—they resisted turning Matt's young life into a media circus.

At one point, someone on each of the local newspapers, several of the television stations, and several national news magazines knew our story but respected our need for confidentiality.

Compassion is often found in unexpected places. Some of the churches did not meet the test as well as did members of the news media.

We braced for discovery when the Paul Michael Glaser family went public about AIDS in their family. One of the stars of the *Starsky and Hutch* television series, Paul was a well-known Hollywood actor. His family's experience with AIDS was similar to that of Scott and Lydia's. Mrs. Glaser was infected at the birth of her child. There was no misconduct on her part; Elizabeth contracted the virus in the hospital. Similar to our family, Paul was clear of the virus, but his wife and two children contracted AIDS.

When rumors surfaced that the Glasers had AIDS, one of the nation's most scandalous tabloid newspapers refused to honor the family's request for privacy. To prevent their story from being misrepresented to the public, the Glasers decided to handle the disclosure by telling their secret to the world in advance of the paper's next edition.

When the Glasers went public, the Hollywood community rallied around them. Together with others who shared their concern, they founded the National Foundation for Pediatric AIDS. Because of their friendship with President Ronald Reagan, they received national support.

Although Elizabeth and one of the children, Ariel, have since died, their story has been one of courage and positive contribution to the cause of helping the helpless. The parents tried to carry the burden of the secret to protect their children, but the seedier side of the press had not allowed them to do so. Yet the Glasers managed to bring good out of what some disreputable members of the press had meant for evil and scandal.

While the Glaser tragedy made headlines and filled airtime, we were thankful for our news friends who remained true to their promises not to run our story.

Long before the Glaser family's exposure, Scott and Lydia and I had talked at length about whether we had a responsibility to tell our story. Our reasoning went something like this: Ignorance and fear are twins. Maybe what we were going through could be instructive and encouraging to others facing similar situations. Perhaps the ultimate good of that possibility outweighed our interest in protecting Matt from awkward or embarrassing situations. Furthermore, Matt might be as well off in an open atmosphere as he was in a protected one. Maybe the secret ought not to be a secret at all.

By this time, Scott and his family had moved to a house in Dallas. Some thoughtful Christians had helped Scott and Lydia purchase the home and repair it. Ironically, the same church who helped Scott and Lydia find a place to live was unwilling to have Matt attend its Sunday school. Nevertheless, our family was deeply grateful for the assistance.

Scott, Lydia, and I sat in the couple's new den and discussed whether we should take the wraps off the secret. Back and forth we went: Should we go public and risk verbal or possible physical persecution? At the very least, we felt we would be ostracized by those more influenced by fear than by facts. On the other hand, we no longer would have to hide, and possibly, some good could come of it. Or, should we continue to keep the secret? Although Lydia was reluctant, she was willing to do whatever would be of greatest help, even to opening her family's life to a documentary film crew, as long as it did not place Matt in any danger.

I offered to call Bill Moyers. Bill is a friend of long-standing, as well as a highly respected person in the media. I knew he would be sensitive to our needs, while offering insight into the positives and negatives of going public with our story. Scott and Lydia knew Bill's keen ability to listen and elicit response from others in documentary fashion, and considered him the best counselor available.

Bill flew to Dallas to talk with Scott and Lydia. They explained their dilemma and told him that although they desired to be neither stars nor martyrs, they wondered if a documentary for television ought to be made of their experiences. Scott and Lydia wondered about the value and risks such a loss of privacy might evoke.

Bill spent an entire day discussing the potential benefits and problems of taking such a route. As Bill talked with Scott and Lydia, he pointed out that the presence of a camera that would make everything that happened public would change the whole nature of their lives. It would add stress to stress.

After thoroughly discussing their options with Bill, Scott and Lydia decided to back away from the idea of a documentary on their life and death with AIDS. They continued, however, to wrestle with how they might help other AIDS victims deal with the disease and its physical, emotional, social, and spiritual ramifications. They decided that doing so, from a public platform at least, would have to wait until Matthew was old enough to handle the public scrutiny.

Choosing when to go public became Scott's task. Lydia had wanted privacy, but by the time of her death in February 1992, our family had harbored the secret for over seven years. The burden was growing heavy. Besides, Scott had worked feverishly along with others to bring the AIDS crisis to the nation's attention. His position with the U.S. Commission on AIDS took him all over the country. It was apparent that the issue needed more attention. His colleagues at the commission asked him to consider telling his story publicly. Scott gave it a great deal of thought, discussed the issue with Matt, then decided to do so.

We were going public.

The questions then were where and when. We went back to our list of reporters who agreed to hold our story. It was now payback time.

Finally, the day arrived. Matt was ten years old. My telephone rang, and before I could get the receiver to my ear, I heard Matt saying excitedly, "Granddad! I don't have a secret anymore. I've gone public!"

I had dreaded that day, but Matt's joy was contagious.

"Well, how do you feel about it?" I asked him.

"Granddad, I feel great!"

I learned something from that telephone call. Containing the secret had been harder for Matt than I had known. All along, he had been free to tell any friend he wanted of his deadly disease. But in four years of school, he had told only three playmates. Now, at last, he was free.

The New York Times broke the story on September 8, 1992. The NBC *Today* show followed. NBC's news magazine program, *Dateline*, made the story a feature. For better or worse, the news media focused on the church's response to our family's experience. Scott handled the questions calmly and without vindictiveness. He simply told the truth, and cited fear as the enemy of compassion.

I was invited to appear along with Scott and Matt on *Dateline*, but I declined. I sensed the producer wanted to slant the story away from Lydia, Matt, and Scott to my relationship with my homosexual son, Skip. I was not about to allow that to happen. It was, after all, Matt's and Scott's story that was most significant, not mine.

I suspected I would be skewered for turning down the interview. I was right. When the story aired, it included an unflattering photo of me, and the ambiguous and misleading statement that I was separated from

Skip by "dogma." If they meant that Skip and I disagreed on his homosexual expression, they were correct; if they meant that we had allowed it to create a
barrier between us, they were wrong. Unfortunately,
the dogma statement, couched in a negative context,
left the viewer uncertain about how Skip and I regarded each other. Most people who watched the show
probably assumed the worst.

An article on Scott and Lydia in *Texas Monthly*,
though, clarified and explained the story so poignantly
that I still hear from people who were helped in their
understanding by reading it. My only regret is that we
could not send copies of the article to all the viewers of
the *Dateline* feature.

One of the positive results of going public with our
story was the opportunity for the Lakewood Elementary School to reveal its attitudes about Matt. Following the revelation that Matt had AIDS, a disease his
mother and brother had died from, the Lakewood Elementary Parents-Teachers Association held a public information meeting featuring Scott and Matt telling
their story and answering questions. Literally all the
parents who attended the meeting expressed their support for Matt. The faculty, as well, signed a statement
of support. That same week, Matt and Scott led a
school assembly where Matt answered questions about
what AIDS is and how it affected him.

Most of his schoolmates' questions were basic. They
wanted to know what AIDS feels like. Matt's answers
were equally down-to-earth.

"I have to go to the bathroom a lot," he said. "And
I feel tired a lot."

Other questions were more philosophical. Some of

the kids wanted to know what it feels like to know that you are dying.

Matt responded, "That's just the way it is. We're all dying. It's only a matter of when."

It appeared that going public with the secret would accomplish its purpose.

There were surprisingly few negative results from revealing the secret. I believe one of the reasons for that was Scott's strategy of direct confrontation and of providing information. Wherever an incident developed—in school, the neighborhood, on the baseball diamond—Scott went immediately to the person involved to provide information and dialogue about AIDS, and particularly, about how the disease affected Matt.

Shortly after the school assembly, for instance, one of Matt's fellow ten year olds began the chant on the playground, "You've got AIDS. You've got AIDS." When Matt came home from school, he told his father about the incident. That evening, Scott confronted the child's parents. It became an occasion for the boy to understand what he had said and why it was wrong. The parents were supportive and eager to help, and the problem was alleviated.

Another result of going public was that the churches that had refused to allow Matt into their Sunday school program were asked by reporters to explain their actions. Most of the church spokespersons skirted the issue—except for Dr. Charles Wade of the First Baptist Church of Arlington, Texas. I consider Charles Wade a friend, and Wanda and I still maintain our Southern Baptist membership in his church. When a reporter asked him to explain his church's rationale for rejecting

Matt, Charles answered with the frank confession, "We blew it."

Since those early rejections, First Baptist, Arlington, as well as each of the other churches that originally refused to admit Matt to Sunday school, has developed programs to minister to people with AIDS and their families. Scores of congregations have contacted these churches to learn what steps to take to reach out to AIDS children. Other congregations have formed AIDS support groups.

Sharing the secret turned out to be less difficult and more productive than we imagined.

SEVENTEEN

"GRANDDAD, DID YOU KNOW I'M DYING?"

MATT HANDLED having AIDS better than the rest of us handled Matt having AIDS. His candid frankness was sometimes disconcerting.

For instance, one day when Matt was six, he and I spent the day together. Because he was in a tree-climbing phase, he regarded any tree nearby and even remotely accessible as a challenge to conquer.

Driving down Hemphill Street in Fort Worth, we spotted a likely tree.

"Let's do that one, Granddad!" Matt said. I pulled the car over to the curb and stopped. We got out to inspect the limbs and accessibility of the tree. A careful climber, Matt studied the possibilities like a mountain climber gauging his chances of scaling Mount Everest.

The decision made, he started his ascent. As a partner in the enterprise, it was my responsibility to shout encouragements and admonitions from the ground.

Matt negotiated each limb, climbing carefully until he reached dizzying heights. He vigilantly called out to me, describing the sights from each perch. I sat on a rock and enjoyed his boyish delight. Little boys live in a world where their line of sight is belt-buckle high. I'm sure Matt enjoyed looking down instead of up all the time. After a while, when Matt felt that he had sufficiently explored all the safe limbs, he climbed down as carefully as he had ascended. We returned to the car to resume our journey toward our original destination and our goal of the moment—Big Macs at McDonald's.

As we drove across a bridge, Matt turned to me and as nonchalantly as if he were asking me the time, he asked, "Granddad, did you know I'm dying?"

His words had the force of a lightning strike. I had known they would come eventually. Matt was too bright not to know he was different. None of the other kids at school received gamma-globulin infusions every three weeks, or took thirty-six pills a day. Matt did.

Other kids could kiss their parents and other family members; Matt could not. In the early days of our experience with AIDS, we were not sure whether the disease was transmitted through contact with saliva. Consequently, Scott and Lydia taught Matt to hug family members and friends, rather than kiss them. Of course, we surrounded Matt with plenty of hugs. We later learned that our no-kissing rule was an unnecessary precaution, but by that time the pattern had become an ingrained part of Matt's personality.

Scott and Lydia had been candid with Matt about most of the details of the disease he was carrying. The one subject all of us within the circle of the secret avoided discussing with him was the inevitability of that disease ending his life. A four or five year old did not have much capacity for understanding death.

Now, as this innocent six-year-old boy looked at me from the passenger's seat, I realized that he was aware that his days on earth were numbered—and that number was much smaller than that of most people. Scott and Lydia obviously had decided it was time to discuss Matt's death with him.

Although I was unprepared for Matt's blunt inquiry concerning his death, it was typical of Matt to open a serious subject out of the blue. He usually mulled things over a long time before letting them surface. Children often engage in foolish chatter to determine whether adults are listening before unloading the important cargo in their minds. Matt did that. Besides, Matt instinctively knew that both his granddad and his papa tended to have several mental tracks going at the same time. Like most children, Matt enjoyed our full attention, and he usually got it.

"Yes, Matt; I know you are dying," I finally mustered the courage to say. "I am dying, too. All of us are dying. The only difference is when we are going to die. We don't know when it will be our time to go. I might die before you do. Probably this disease will make you die before I do. But we all die. Is that scary to you?"

"Yes. But I'll get to see Bryan."

"That's true. He is with God in heaven. He's waiting for you. The two of you will have a good time together. Then one of these days, I'll be there with you. We all will be."

That seemed to satisfy Matt for the moment, and we

moved on to more mundane topics. That conversation, however, altered the tone of our lives. From that day on, death hung as a backdrop for each scene, whether we acknowledged its presence or not. Once mentioned, it could not be ignored. It popped into view from time to time, usually at Matt's initiative.

Matt usually signaled that he wanted to talk about his dying by bringing up Bryan's death. Sometimes Matt would say he missed Bryan, although Matt was barely three years old when Bryan died. Bryan had lived only eight months. Regardless, Matt felt close to his baby brother, and any mention of Bryan became a clue to us that Matt was contemplating his own death. Such hints provided us an opportunity to talk about the subject without worrying that we were unduly dwelling upon it.

I sometimes worried that Bryan's death had become an obsession in the rituals Scott and Lydia had created about him. Lydia's book *I Miss My Baby Brother* had set the tone for Matt's processing of the grief his family was feeling. The regular introduction of Bryan into family talk, as well as all the discussions concerning "Bryan's House," seemed to me to have the potential for a morbid backlash later in Matt's life. The wisdom of Scott and Lydia's plan to prepare Matt for dying became clear to me as we dealt with Lydia's death. Matt had a lot of death to live with.

Matt was amazingly brave in dealing with the pain AIDS brought to his body. During the early days of our secret, I went to visit him one day at the Children's Hospital in Fort Worth. It was a mild winter day, but a chill swept over me as I walked up the stairs of the hospital. I hunched inside my coat and tried to still my heart as I was headed for the ward where my enthusiastic, often laughing, three-year-old grandson coped with another battery of tests and shots. He was registered under an assumed name—the secret had begun.

I reached Matt's bedside as the doctors and nurses left, their blood-gathering chores completed. Large tears glistened on Matt's cheeks. "Matt, what's wrong?" I asked.

He said, "Granddad, I'm not very brave."

I reached down to hug him and said, "Why, Matt? Why do you say you're not very brave?"

"The doctor kept telling me, 'Be brave, be brave,' but I'm not very brave."

I stood at Matt's bedside, soothing him, but inside I was boiling. This child, born in a crisis of life and death, had already been through three operations. He probably had experienced more pain in his three years than that doctor or I had known in a lifetime. I had never spent a night in a hospital as a patient. But as a pastor, husband, and father, I had visited a lot of medical institutions. I wondered how many times the doctor had been flat on his back, while being punctured repeatedly with needles.

"Matt," I said, "you are the bravest person I have ever known. You're brave, baby, you *are* brave."

When I calmed down, I went to talk with that doctor. He had meant to encourage Matt. The doctor honestly did not realize the discouraging impact his words had on his patient. Matt did not even know what brave meant. But he lived it. After the doctor and I discussed the matter, he never again asked Matt to be brave.

I once heard Lydia say to a doctor, "I have a baby with the highest pain threshold you've ever seen." I believe it. I have been with him dozens of times for his "big owie." That was what Matt called his gamma globulin intravenous injection that he received every three weeks of his life. I watched him as a five year old in his playroom, towing around that glucose bottle hanging from a metal tree on wheels. Matt played contentedly, virtually ignoring the tube stuck in a vein in his arm.

In his eleventh year, Matt suffered violent bouts of vomiting, often in the middle of the night. He usually dealt with it himself. Once, however, I was in the bathroom with him, ready with a glass of water so he could wash out his mouth. Between heaves, Matt looked up and said in his flat conversational way, "I am definitely not feeling well today." I nearly broke up. Brave? I wish I was that brave.

Later, Matt had to have some minor surgery as part of his treatment. Of course, no surgery is ever minor for an AIDS patient. The doctors clipped some tissue from his intestine and his stomach wall, in hopes of discovering whether the wasting away of his body was caused primarily by the virus that takes the lives of most AIDS patients, or by something else. As I talked to him the next day, I asked, "Matt, are you hurting?"

"No, Granddad. I have some minor abdominal pain, but I'm all right. I'm just tired."

Other kids have stomachaches. Matt had "minor abdominal pain." The words *I'm just tired* became a theme of his life.

Living with Matt's death in our peripheral vision made it essential that our family live each day in the present tense. Early on in our AIDS crisis, Wanda and I decided we would take life one day at a time. We treasure the memories of the past, but we dwell on life each day.

Knowing that Matt's time with us was limited, we set about cramming a lifetime of experiences into little more than a decade. Travel was one of Matt's favorite activities. In fact, he was so fascinated by the Statue of Liberty, that he wanted to see it and climb it. Since I had a lot of business in New York City, I arranged to take Matt with me on a trip to the Big Apple.

We had a long delay at DFW airport and decided to relax in the Delta Club, an airport home away from home for many frequent travelers. As we got on the elevator to the Delta Airlines concourse, Matt asked, "Will this make our flight any faster?" The boy was ready to go!

It was after midnight when we finally arrived at our hotel in New York. I was tired and ready for bed. Not Matt. His adrenaline pumped so strongly, he would have jumped on the boat for Ellis Island right then, if I had allowed him.

I knew Matt was excited, but I was unprepared for the fierce determination of that strong-willed child. He intended to climb to the top of the Lady of Liberty to look out at the world. I tried to convince him that the lower platforms were enough. They may have been enough for me, but not for Matt. To the bemusement of our fellow tourists, he climbed every step to the top! I was delighted that he was unwilling to settle for less. He had to have help getting down, but he did the hardest part by himself. Matt's trek up the stairs of the Statue became a cherished memory for him, and a tale I still delight in telling.

I was, however, a little embarrassed when he asked the doorman at the United Nations Hotel if he had ever been to the Statue. When the doorman sheepishly confessed he had not visited the site, Matt lectured him about his neglect. It was quite a scene as this little child put his hands on his hips, looked up at the tall door-man, and said, "You mean you are right across from the Statue of Liberty and you have never even gone over there? You need to go see it."

The doorman held his hands up in mock surrender and said, "Okay. Okay. I'll go. I'll go."

That wasn't enough for Matt. "When?" he demanded to know.

"On my day off next week."

Mollified, Matt said, "Well, you'd better."

Unfortunately, Matt never returned to New York to check whether the doorman kept his promise. Someday, I may stop by the hotel to see if I can locate that doorman.

Matt and I became travel partners when he was only three months old. Lydia was determined to bring her firstborn from California to Texas for Christmas dinner with her family. I promised Lydia that Matt would not cry on his first airplane ride. Sure enough, I held him as he slept contentedly all the way from San Francisco to the Dallas–Fort Worth airport. Months later, Matt uttered his first complete sentence—on an airplane, where else? As the flight attendant passed by with the beverage cart, Matt spoke demurely but clearly, "Could I have some more apple juice, please?"

Matt and I stored up the travel memories, including Hawaii's beaches, Disney World, Washington, Williamsburg, and on and on. One of Matt's all-time favorite travel experiences took place the last year before his mama died. Matt went to the Cayman Islands with Scott and Lydia. When they returned home, Matt could hardly stop talking about his swim among the stingrays, the clarity of the water, and the joy of the beach. The Cayman Island trip had provided a God-created setting in which three battered people found a much needed respite.

Another favorite of the dozens of places Matt and I have been together is Maui. As we flew to Honolulu, before taking another flight to the outer islands, the flight attendant told Matt he could go into the cockpit after the landing. Matt and another boy about his age did so. Sitting in the pilot's seat, talking to the air traffic control tower, and touching the controls of the jetliner all added up to an unforgettable experience for Matt. Later, when we took a helicopter ride into Maui's lush mountainside where we saw the volcanic valley and beautiful waterfalls, he drank it all in. Later his delight was boundless when he recognized the landscape that provided the setting for the movie *Jurassic Park*. When we visited Maui, Matt still was robust enough to enjoy the beach, trips in the large catamaran, and snorkeling in the clear Pacific water—all this, with a McDonald's only seven minutes away!

Despite his constant battle with the disease in his body, Matt was a normal boy in every sense of the word. If someone asked him what he wanted to be when he grew up, Matt's list might include an actor, a stand-up comedian, a marine biologist, or a video game critic. After Wanda and I moved to the mountains of Georgia, Matt's university loyalty was to Georgia Tech. His favorite baseball team was the Atlanta Braves. He remained unswervingly loyal to the Dallas Cowboys throughout his lifetime. He treasured his Elton John autograph, even though his favorite group was the Beach Boys. In his bedroom hung the boxing gloves worn by Muhammad Ali while he trained for three world championship bouts.

Toys 'R' Us was Matt's favorite place for shopping or browsing. If you are going to be a video game critic—analyzing how to improve or create them—you have to be up on each new development. He was quick to tell whether a game was "awesome!" or "borrrrring!"

As much as Matt and I enjoyed Toys 'R' Us, we both were frustrated when the company's chairman of the board failed to acknowledge our letter suggesting a Christmas season sales idea that we called "Kidsperts." While browsing in the video game section one day, Matt and I encountered a bewildered mother trying to figure out what to buy her ten-year-old son. Since Matt and I were standing nearby, she asked me for help. I referred her to my kid expert, and Matt walked her through the decision. The woman was so grateful for our help, Matt and I decided we had come up with something—having kids advise adults on which toys kids really liked.

We brainstormed how our kid experts, Kidsperts, could be selected in a contest, trained in manners, dressed in Toys 'R' Us jackets, and employed during Christmas seasons on three-hour shifts. We suggested all this in our letter to the company CEO, as well as suggesting that the Kidsperts be paid in Toys 'R' Us money, and helped to learn merchandising.

It sounded like a fantastic idea, but no answer came, not even "thanks, but no thanks." Matt was more than a little disappointed by the lack of response of his favorite store to our idea.

As Matt's strength diminished, he could not do many of the active little boy things he did only a few years before. Video games and movies filled the vacuum in his life. Matt became a walking encyclopedia in both fields. Besides helping him to pass the many hours of nonphysical activity, they made handy escapes from the stress and pain of AIDS.

It is not surprising that movies and television intrigued Matt. After all, his grandmother was a drama major, his grandfather produced television programs, his uncle performed on the stage, and his father is a public communicator. More than that, however, a movie theater became a place of refuge and a resource center for Matt. He never left the theater until all the credits had run. He wanted to know who did what to make the movie work.

The breakdown of community in our society has caused us to have fewer and fewer common experiences out of which to examine life. Television and movies create that common denominator, and people in those fields often venture meaningfully into life's deepest questions. Consequently, in my preaching, I use a lot of illustrations from the world of art and drama. It delighted Matt when I called to ask him the name of an actor or a movie I wanted to use in a sermon illustration. He was a walking reference library on G- and PG-rated movies.

Often Matt's familiarity with TV and movies provided natural occasions for talking about values. For example, Matt and I discussed emotional depression and suicidal impulses after watching a movie about a convict on parole who got hit by a car and woke up as an apprentice angel. The theology of the film was terrible, but it was not a time to discuss theological correctness.

As he pondered the implications of the movie, Matt said to me, "Granddad, sometimes I wish a truck would hit me the same way."

We talked about the reasons for living as long as he could: the people who loved him and enjoyed him, the fact that we stay alive not so much because we are afraid to die but because we love life here with our friends and family members, and because of the good

things we can count on with God present and available
to us.

In my weakest moments, I wondered why God would
allow such a great kid as Matt to be born, only to take
him away from us. I refuse to dwell on such questions.
I was helped immensely by an article written by my
friend Michael Gartner in his July 5, 1994 *USA Today*
column about the sudden death of his seventeen-year-
old son. Michael cited a conversation with a North
Carolina friend who helped him deal with his son's ab-
breviated life. The friend proposed, "If God had come
to you seventeen years ago and said, 'I'll make you a
bargain. I'll give you a beautiful, wonderful, happy kid
for seventeen years and then I'll take him away,' you
would have made that deal in a second."

As I read Michael's column, my mind was flooded
with memories of Matt—pain and pleasure, anxieties
and relief, "need-a-hug" experiences, and the anticipation of being together again. I thought, *He's right. The
deal would be gladly accepted. It's worth it and more.*

As for Matt, if there was an award for being an eternal optimist, he would have won it long ago. Once, he
and Wanda walked across a field together. Wanda an-
chored a bobbing, helium-filled balloon, the last rem-
nant of a birthday party they had attended. A sudden
gust of wind swept the balloon out of Wanda's hand.
She exclaimed, "Oh, Matt, I'm sorry. I lost the balloon." They tried to recapture it, but it got away.

As they watched it rise on the wind, Matt said,
"Don't worry about it, Grandma. Momma and Bryan
will take care of it."

EIGHTEEN

TOUGH
TRANSITIONS

SHORTLY BEFORE LYDIA'S DEATH, I sensed a time of transition coming for Wanda and me. We still lived in Fort Worth, but I had resigned my position as director of the Radio and Television Commission with the ACTS Network, and had moved to more of a consulting role within the Southern Baptist Convention. Although ostensibly semiretired, I was busier than ever. I served as a consultant for several universities, and I preached every Sunday at the First Baptist Church in Amarillo, Texas. The congregation of about four thousand people was searching for a new pastor, so in the interim, I preached weekly for them. Every Sunday morning, I flew to Amarillo from Fort Worth, or wherever else I was working around the country.

In addition to these responsibilities, I headed an overseas missions committee and consulted on fundraising for other philanthropic causes. I was not looking for a new challenge.

Consequently, when I was invited to become preaching chaplain of the chapel in Big Canoe, Georgia, a mountain resort community about fifty miles north of Atlanta, I was hesitant about accepting. Our family and my vocational root system were in Texas. Besides, Lydia was close to death; Matt was sick, as well, and the idea of moving over a thousand miles away when they might need us the most did not appeal to Wanda and me.

Yet I felt that sense of light the Spirit of God always gave me when he guided me to some particular task. All the signs of his presence pointed me toward the mountains of Big Canoe, Georgia. The door of opportunity opened without my having to find the door, much less force it open.

As much as possible, I stayed close to Dallas so I could be available to Scott and Matt. It was a mystery to me why God put it in my heart to move to Georgia, and why God put it in the hearts of the spiritual leaders at Big Canoe to invite me to minister there. I was the least likely person to be called to pastor their cross-denominational group of people. Usually such groups are not likely to call a person who has been involved in denominational ministry as much as I have. Although I ministered outside my own denomination, that was not my forte.

Consequently, when the Father lay this new calling in my heart, I was staggered. Wanda, too, was surprised that I would consider moving at this point in our lives. Wanda's reluctance to move, however, was not unusual. Throughout our years of marriage and ministry, every time I sensed God moving me to a new area of ministry, Wanda moved with me, crying all the way, with her heels dug into the pavement. We have never moved without Wanda feeling reluctant to leave.

The idea of moving from the flatlands of Fort Worth to the mountains of Georgia was astounding to her. We had visited Big Canoe several times and she always enjoyed the brief getaway to the mountains, but the idea of us living there, as long as Lydia and Matt were still with us, seemed ludicrous to Wanda.

Our friend Wayne Smith, who served on the board of the college in Thailand with me, lived in Big Canoe. Wayne was assistant chaplain at the church there. Because my work with the television network frequently took me to Atlanta, I often spent the night with Wayne and his family. One weekend when I was visiting, Wayne said, "Since you are here, would you preach for us?" I said that I would be glad to preach at the chapel, and Wayne smiled slyly. He had in mind the whole time that I should be chaplain there.

That Sunday morning I experienced for the first time the chapel service and its nondenominational approach to worship and ministry. For a seasoned soldier like me, war torn and battle weary from years of denominational skirmishes, it was refreshing to simply focus on God and his love, without all the excess baggage. The congregation at the chapel was several hundred strong, dynamic, eclectic, and made up almost entirely of people who had come from a rich church experience someplace else.

After several months of conversation with Wayne about my availability, I went to Big Canoe to visit with Dr. Vernon Broyles, the founder of Big Canoe Chapel and a man whose spiritual stature and wisdom I greatly respected. During my visit, Dr. Broyles told me why I ought to be the next chaplain at Big Canoe. I finally agreed that Wanda and I would come visit with their pastoral search committee.

Back home, when I broached the subject to Wanda, and asked her to visit with the committee, she stared at me, and said, "You don't really mean this?"

I said, "Yes, I am talking seriously."

"All right," she said, "I will go, but don't expect too much."

Wanda and I flew into Atlanta the night before our visit with the committee from Big Canoe Chapel. The following morning, we drove out to Big Canoe, stopping to get some breakfast on the way. We were sitting in the restaurant when Wanda said, "I can't do this."

"Okay," I said, "I will call the committee chairman right now and tell them we cannot come."

Wanda's expression registered her surprise. She said, "You will do that?" Wanda was not accustomed to me changing my mind so easily.

"That is one of the things I talked to the Father about," I explained. "This situation is so unusual that we can't rely only on my sense of God's leadership; you have to feel it, as well. If you don't sense that God wants us to move out here, then we are going back home. That is a part of the test. There is no use dragging you through all of this if God is not leading both of us."

Wanda could hardly believe her ears. I had never before been so pliable as we sought the will of God about an opportunity. In the past, as I sensed the direction of God, I told Wanda what I felt we must do. Frequently, she did not like it when we first moved to another area, but then she grew accustomed to the new location, accepted it, and learned to love it.

But this time it was different. Wanda's change of at-

titude toward the move came as she made the trip to
Georgia. She insisted on driving her own car from Fort
Worth to Big Canoe. She needed the uninterrupted
time. Still resistant deep inside about moving that far
away from Matt, nevertheless she prayed as she drove.
Somehow she took a wrong turn, and wandered
through Elijay, Georgia, a beautiful area. During that
detour, God gave Wanda peace in her heart that this
move was right. By the time she arrived in Big Canoe,
the matter was settled in her heart and mind. It didn't
hurt that Wanda met the people and immediately felt
their love. By the end of the trip, she was certain this
was where God wanted us to be.

Wanda needed the type of accepting, supporting
community that Big Canoe Chapel provided. In Fort
Worth, she was the wife of an executive of a major
ministry. She had many friends, and many people who
looked to her for help and encouragement, but she had
no network in which she could be nurtured. The people of Big Canoe did not see her as the president's wife
or the pastor's wife, they simply loved and accepted
Wanda as herself, a woman who had suffered much
hurt and grief and needed someone to put an arm
around her once in a while and let her know that it was
worth it to keep going on and to keep on believing for
God's best.

For me, Big Canoe was a breath of fresh air—in
more ways than one. At three thousand feet above sea
level, the mountaintop to which Wanda and I moved
boasts some of the best views in the Appalachian
Mountain chain. A resort community, Big Canoe provides plenty of fishing, golfing, swimming, and hiking.
In many ways, it is a gorgeous retreat from the world.
And yet, its people are actively engaged in the world,

not simply as businesspersons, parents, and grandparents, but as Christians.

As I look back on it now, I can see that God gave my family and me a beautiful gift. He put us in a place of solace, but also a place of usefulness and fulfillment, surrounded by the natural beauty he created where we could struggle through our painful journey.

A gratifying, unexpected part of God's provision for us was that Big Canoe became a haven for Matt.

Lydia and Scott worked hard to create rituals of play and cheerfulness in Matt's life. One of the most enjoyable of these was what they called *rowdy night*. Since Matt was old enough to remember, he and Scott had one night a week that belonged only to them. The two would rent movies, eat pizza, romp, play, and laugh. The house belonged to them. Normally, they did it on Friday night, as a way to finish the work week. Sometimes rowdies took the form of special nights out: either a visit to Six Flags Over Texas or a baseball or basketball game. Pillow fights were permissible on rowdy night. Sometimes a friend was allowed to stay over. Mayhem ruled on rowdy night. So did laughter, and with it the healing of the heart.

Matt and I had our own version of rowdy night. We call it *just us guys*. We started doing just-us-guy things as part of our weekly adventure to a playground at McDonald's. No women-folk were allowed. This was time for Matt and me to be together and to do all the things that little boys—and grandfathers with a lot of little boy in them—love to do. We went to parks, museums, and all sorts of other places. Both Matt and I looked forward to *just us guys*.

*   *   *

When we first moved to the Georgia mountains, Wanda stayed behind in Texas for several weeks to close up our house and to work with the realtor, while I began my duties as chaplain at Big Canoe. School was out for the summer in Texas, so I talked Scott into letting Matt come to Georgia with me for a visit. Matt and I lived like bachelors in our new house, and we explored every nook and cranny of our mountain resort. We had two weeks of uninterrupted pleasure.

We went swimming every day. We found the Lower Falls, a gorgeous spot where a mountain stream turns into a waterfall. We hiked the nature trail. We took turns going down the rock slide at the swim club. In a single afternoon Matt went down the regular water slide sixty-eight times, laughing each and every time.

On that first visit, Matt and I started the tradition of the world's greatest two-man checker tournament with daily sessions of intense competition at the old-fashioned Country Store in Big Canoe. Sitting on barrels like the old-timers used to do, Matt and I battled it out for checker supremacy. Matt became the talk of the mountain. In checkers, at least, he always won.

Big Canoe became a sanctuary for Matt. It was a place where he could get out of the city, away from all the bad memories he had known in Dallas, and simply enjoy God's beautiful creation. One day as we rode down the Jeep trail, he said, "Granddad, this is a little boy's paradise."

I replied, "Matt, that is true, and it's a granddad's paradise too." I was glad Wanda and I had dared to make the tough transition to Big Canoe.

In the meantime, Scott went through a time of transition, as well.

Scott's loneliness began long before Lydia died. Estranged from her world toward the end of her life, Lydia stepped into and out of Scott's world on a regular basis. None of our family members, including Scott, held it against her; the disease with which we were living and Lydia was dying blurred all semblances of normal life. Still, it was hard for Scott to understand some of Lydia's actions and attitudes. The couple coped with Matt's needs, struggled with the economic burdens, sought ways of plugging insurance gaps, and communicated well on the essentials. But that was about it.

Scott's energy was tapped out by the strain of constantly caring for Matt, while assisting Lydia when she called on him. When Lydia died, Scott felt a curious mixture of grief and relief. Now he had the responsibility of raising a son without a mother.

We were concerned to see Scott's stamina dwindle; he was drained physically, emotionally, and spiritually. Burnout loomed near. As he became more and more engaged in his work at Southwestern Medical School in Dallas, where he was now employed, Scott drifted away from his only network of Christian support, the caring, compassionate people at the Christian Life Commission. Scott substituted a twelve-step-type support group for their fellowship.

Scott maintained weekly contact with his brother Skip. Skip often stayed over at Scott's house on Sundays, to give Scott a break. Similarly, whenever I could arrange my schedule to go through Dallas, I always allowed extra time for Matt and me to have a just-us-guys experience, so Scott could have some time for himself.

Scott's commitment to Matt was intense; he was one of the best fathers I had seen. But he was lonely.

I was glad when Scott began spending time with Mary Reisinger, a lovely woman in her late thirties.

Mary had been a manager of a furniture business. She understood some of Scott's burden, because Mary struggled with health problems herself. A deer tick bite had infected her with Lyme disease, an inflammatory disease that can cause serious problems if untreated. Not surprisingly, in their mutual pain, Mary and Scott were drawn to each other. To Matt, Mary became "Mareski." Several months later, Matt called me one day and said, "Granddad, Papa and I have decided to marry Mareski."

Blonde, blue-eyed, and petite, Mary made a lovely bride. The ceremony was performed by Larry James, pastor of the Church of Christ in Richardson. Larry had been the one pastor in the Dallas area who took Matt in when Scott tried to place him in a summer program. Larry was well-educated, erudite, personable, and caring. When he and Scott first met, Scott ministered to AIDS victims through the Christian Life Commission, and Larry guided a growing congregation in ministry. Without retreating from his biblical base, Larry reached out to others in the journey and joined in helping hurting people in the name of Christ. Scott instantly was impressed by Larry's genuine Christian compassion.

Larry's church had an excellent day-care center. Like many private schools, it operated on parental paid tuition. As such, it was dependent upon parent approval and participation. Nevertheless, when Larry found out Matt needed a day school for the summer, he unhesitatingly invited him. He issued a letter to his church and interested parents that said, "This is to declare our day school an AIDS zone." He went on to explain the nature of the ministry and the decision to accept Matt. He told me later that he didn't lose a single child from his program as a result. Moreover, he had a number of opportunities to help educate parents, church members, and other interested individuals about AIDS.

Larry's attitude both encouraged and depressed me. On the one hand, I was delighted to find a pastor who recognized the need and the possibility of ministering to AIDS families. On the other hand, I yearned for a chance to roll back the calendar to those days of our frantic search for a Sunday school that would accept Matt. My heart ached to have a chance to recover what my children had lost in their disillusionment.

Scott and Mary's marriage ceremony was a model in overcoming prejudices. Mary's family overcame their Roman Catholic reservations to the marriage. I put aside my own biases. Larry James ministered to all of us.

Matthew was ring bearer. His new shoes pinched his feet, but he grimaced his way into them. He made it down the aisle and onto the platform. But his sharp-eyed grandmother saw him slip out of them and stand in his stocking feet throughout the wedding rituals.

During the ceremony, Scott and Mary made several new vows to each other. One vow they took, however, was a classic. It was a parent's vow, made by Scott and Mary to Matt. Created by them for the occasion, it said:

> Matthew,
> With all our heart and soul
> we dedicate ourselves to you.
> The Eternal has honored us
> with the task of guiding you
> in the ways of the heart.

We encourage you to explore
the depths of your soul
the height of your spirit,
and to follow the path of your heart
in your eternal quest
to experience the gift of life.

We promise
to the best of our ability
to share this journey with you
with love and support,
gentleness and kindness,
and a faithfulness to the Center of Life itself.
We accept the honor of being your parents.
And as one family
we devote our lives
to the celebration of life;
to sharing our laughter and joy,
our pain and our sorrow
and our courage and strength.
We leave this place as one
and take our place on the sacred path.

After those beautiful words and the presentation of the bride and groom, there was a mad scramble by a little boy in a sharp tuxedo to get back into his shoes before leaving the platform! They had succeeded in "marrying Mareski."

Overcoming loneliness helped, but it did not solve Scott's burnout. The problem intensified about a year later, when it became apparent that Matt's health was slipping rapidly. Scott's understanding bosses at the medical school let him work from home, but he had trouble keeping up with his work while caring for

Matt. Both Scott's and Mary's exhaustion levels were reaching an alarming point.

Scott and Mary decided to take a family leave, as allowed under the new federal law, and spend it at Big Canoe. It meant a temporary end to Scott's regular income, but he and Mary rightly recognized that they would need some recovery time before facing the next phase of Matt's ordeal with AIDS.

NINETEEN

MATT'S DOWNHILL SLIDE

MANY PEOPLE who develop full-blown AIDS die within one year of getting sick. Some die within two years of contracting the disease. Nearly all die within ten years of developing the disease. As far as our family was concerned, every day that Matt lived was a blessing.

Despite the AIDS he carried in his body, Matt's first eleven years were full of all the usual little boy fun. He played Little League baseball, for example, in Dallas. He bubbled with enthusiasm, even if his energy level was low. He loved to play practical jokes, especially on his granddad, and his laugh was more contagious than the disease he carried. Matt brought happiness to everyone who knew him.

By 1994, however, his health seriously deteriorated.

He was tired most of the time. Diarrhea and nausea plagued him daily. He returned to school after summer vacation, but often was unable to make it through an entire day of classes. Many days he was too weak to attend school at all. Matt never complained about his condition, although with a smile on his face and a twinkle in his eye he sometimes lamented that he "had to miss math."

During the summer of 1994, we became painfully aware that Matt would not live much longer. His body became so weak that it could no longer extract nutrition from the food he ate. His doctors tried all sorts of modern nutritional wonders, hoping they would sustain him. None did.

Matt's body wasted away during the early fall, and we expected his death before the Thanksgiving and Christmas holidays. His weight continued to drop, plummeting to fifty-eight pounds. His body simply could not get enough nourishment. With the diarrhea and nausea, his food exited his body before it could provide any nutritional value to him. His appetite disappeared. The end seemed near.

But God gave us an unexpected reprieve.

During a trip to Greece in the early spring, I met Ed Noble, an Atlanta businessman. Ed had heard about Matt. One day, while on board our ship, Ed told me of an investment he had made in a company that produced a nutritional substance that helped AIDS patients near the end of their lives.

I liked Ed and was interested in what he had to say, but I was wary of his product. During our eight years of living with AIDS, we had been approached by people touting all kinds of supposed cures and quick fixes. Most were pipe dreams at best, and some were blatant rip-offs. But when we investigated the product in which

Ed had invested, we found people indeed were helped by it. It was not a cure, but it was a help.

Ed helped us secure the supplement for Matt. For a time, Matt's energy increased significantly and his appetite improved. Soon, however, it became apparent that the supplement would not be enough.

Matt's doctor, Janet Squires, suggested one last radical action. A plastic tube, or shunt, was surgically inserted directly into Matt's heart, so liquid nutrition could be fed straight into Matt's blood stream, bypassing his digestive system entirely. Each night while Matt slept, nutrients flowed into his body through the heart shunt. During the day, the shunt was unhooked so Matt could move around, although the tubes still dangled from his chest and were visible beneath his shirt. When Matt needed nutrition during the day, a backpack with shoulder straps allowed him to carry the bag of nutrients around. It was heart-wrenching to watch Matt patiently go through the process of being hooked up to his food source and then move carefully to his television or other activities, all with the disease's horrible pain racking his body. Yet he endured without complaint.

At least one part of Matt's experience was a dieter's dream. He could eat anything he wanted, and as much as he wanted. The food had no bearing on his body— positively or negatively.

Because of the direct feeding of nutrients, his body began to pick up weight. He was puffy and swollen, but his weight increased to seventy-three pounds—more than he had ever weighed! His face lost the sunken, skull-like look that he had taken on during the early part of the wasting process. The round face that resulted from the medication was not exactly a source of encouragement. His facial features had a sickly look.

His body movements were stiff and difficult. Nevertheless, as we approached the holiday season, Matt was still alive, and we were grateful.

Matt's great desire was to come to Big Canoe's mountains one more time. Thanksgiving provided the occasion. Matt, Mary, and Scott came to Georgia for the holiday. It was a poignant and precious time.

Matt and I rode up and down the mountains. We visited our favorite spots, and played a final game of checkers at the Country Store. Matt won, of course.

We saw waterfalls, deer, and lakes. As we looked at the lake where Matt and I had gone swimming so many times during his first trip to Big Canoe, I reminded him of the day he and a buddy had a contest to see how many times they could go down the water slide. Matt made it more than sixty times.

As Matt looked longingly at the water slide, he said quietly, "Boy, I couldn't do it one time now."

He asked if he could say grace at the Thanksgiving meal. I assured him he could, but when the time came, he was too sick to pray.

Wanda and I offered to relieve Scott and Mary of the constant responsibility of caring for Matt. We wanted to give the stressed-out couple a bit of emotional breathing time. Unfortunately, they felt that connecting and disconnecting the heart shunt was too delicate a process to turn over to someone else. Their recreational time had to be squeezed between heart shunt connections.

Despite the unusual circumstances, Wanda and I found plenty of time to be with Matt; we all shared lots of hugging and loving. Thanksgiving is gratitude time, and we were thankful that Matt could be with us at all.

*   *   *

Christmas was another gift. Matt's physical condition continued to deteriorate despite the feedings through the heart shunt. It was impossible for him to come to Big Canoe, so Wanda and I went to Dallas. As the family gathered, a cloud of finality hung over us. Everyone knew this most likely would be Matt's last Christmas. Holidays are bittersweet when death stands at the door.

Matt heroically tried to make it a good Christmas for all. He responded appreciatively to each Christmas gift he received. His comments—"Oh, thank you. I really needed that!" or "That is just what I wanted!"—seemed paradoxical though. His desire for material things had ebbed to the point that it was difficult for us to get him anything that made any sense. After all, what sort of gift do you give a child who is incapacitated and could die at any moment? Finally, Wanda and I settled on a television set and videocassette recorder for Matt's room. He could work the remote control from his bed and watch and rewatch the programs of his choice. It was perfect.

A few days before we arrived for the holidays, seven of Matt's teachers and his school principal took him to a steakhouse in north Dallas. It was such a treat for Matt that he wanted to return to that restaurant with us. When we got there, the maitre d' recognized him and seated us immediately. Matt ordered the best steak in the house, and ate every bit of it. Afterward, Matt wanted to browse in a store next to the restaurant that specialized in muscle relaxation products—hospital beds, special pillows, heat pads, and the sort. He purchased a neck pillow and a chemical heat pack for muscle pain relief.

I remembered the hundreds of just-us-guys days when we had browsed through Toys 'R' Us for power figures, video games, and other toys. It was a mark of Matt's journey that his browsing now centered on pain and its relief.

We did our best to shake off morbid thoughts and celebrate Christmas as usual, but much of our merriment was artificial. Bryan was dead. Luke was dead. Lydia was dead, and Matt was dying. It was useless to pretend that everything was okay. I kept reminding myself that it was a gift to have Matt with us at twelve years of age. I had thought he, too, would be gone long before now.

The day after we arrived back in Big Canoe from the Christmas holiday visit was a disaster for Matt. The nutrition he received through the heart shunt had adversely affected his liver. It had swollen severely, and pressed against his spleen, causing a sudden jaundice. Matt was rushed to the hospital with a high fever. Ironically, it could have been fatal.

The decision was made to stop the feeding, and almost immediately Matt's temperature receded. His liver returned to normal size. Tests were run and it was discovered that Matt's body was overrun by HIV. All of his vital organs had been invaded by the virus. Matt's heartbeat was racing at 163 beats per minute. The doctors said he could not possibly survive much longer. At best, it would only be a matter of weeks.

Wanda and I had barely unpacked our suitcases when Scott called to give us the disappointing news. We decided to return to Texas immediately. We packed fresh clothes and drove straight through from Georgia to Texas. We felt that if we could be of help to Scott and Mary, it was reason enough to go. Our real motive, however, was to be with Matt and to have our personal closings with him, if possible.

As Matt's health failed, Scott had to make another hard decision: should he allow Matt's life to be prolonged by artificial means? He and I talked about it, and as difficult as it was, we both recognized that we had come to the end of the line. As Scott and I talked at the hospital, he asked himself more than me, Do we want to do any more interventions? Clinically, there is nothing more they can do for this child. He is going to die. Whether he dies a little later after we have kept him alive artificially with technology and medications, or whether he dies normally is the only question. In both Scott's and my mind, the issue was clear. We wanted Matt to die with dignity, without a bunch of machines prolonging his agony.

"Unhook the shunt," Scott said quietly but firmly.

I nodded my head. No words were necessary. The next move was up to God.

The shunt feedings were stopped. The hospice staff was called in to oversee Matt's dying. The only medicine Matt received from that point on was a pill to help his pancreas function and a pain pill. Morphine patches also were applied regularly to help curb his pain.

The cessation of the medications freed Matt of many of the toxic side effects of the drugs themselves. His liver began to function as normally as an AIDS-ridden liver can. His heartbeat stabilized. After three weeks, Matt's condition had stabilized, so Wanda and I returned to the mountains, but remained on call.

The long wait continued. Matt's strength ebbed away, day after day, inexorably and deliberately. Oxygen tubes long enough to make him ambulatory around the house helped keep his breathing steady. He could leave the oxygen for a few hours at a time. He took a heavy concentration of it before doing so. That allowed Matt to enjoy going to the movies, when he was able.

God must have a sense of humor when it comes to man's arrogance about our knowledge and technology. The best of man's wisdom offered Matt only a few more weeks of life. All the artificial means of prolonging Matt's life left him with no hope. Yet once the medical interventions were stopped, Matt continued to live, not just three weeks, but months, and more! He knew he moved toward death, yet his will to live was so strong he kept pushing back the approaching darkness, one day at a time.

As the weeks of waiting turned into months, Wanda and I made more frequent trips to Dallas. One evening at the house with Matt, while Scott and Mary were out, became a memorable moment for me, a mental image I will cherish for the remainder of my life. Matt and I watched a television program, sitting side by side on the couch. He leaned his head against my shoulder and fell fast asleep. I sat there, still as a stone as he slept, not wanting to move for fear I would disturb him. Minutes ticked by. Then an hour. An hour and a half elapsed with me sitting there motionless and Matt lost in quiet slumber. I was comforted by the warmth of his presence, even as he moved forward on his journey toward death.

Memories rolled through my mind of rollicking times when this wan, slender, hollow-cheeked boy was once robust and laughing. I remembered the time on the fort at Disney World as he rushed from side to side firing the cannons at imaginary enemies. There were the snorkeling days when he shouted with delight over the fish and coral. I heard mental echoes from the past of the squeals and taunts of challenge to Granddad as Matt went down the water slide in our mountain swimming area. The daily checker games at the Country Store flashed across my mind. It was difficult to fathom, but during all of those good times, the death-dealing virus was doing its devious work in Matt's body.

But this child had drunk life to its fullest. He lived with intensity and courage as he met life's challenges. And now he slumbered quietly as AIDS was winning the battle for his body, but not the battle for his spirit. He was a winner in the things that count.

Since Matt first started to school, one of his best friends was a boy named Billy. The summer before Matt's health began to go downhill, Billy and his parents moved to Ohio. Matt and Billy stayed in touch both by telephone and by occasional letters. Writing was not the first choice for either of them.

Billy's telephone number occupied a prominent place in Matt's wristwatch-computer, where he stored all his important telephone numbers. As we sat together at his home one evening, early in the deterioration stage, Matt said, "I wish I could talk to Billy, but I can't call long distance unless Papa is here."

I volunteered my credit card.

I only heard one side of the conversation, but it sounded like two boys talking about what they had done, what games they played, and of course, how terrible school was.

Then as straightforwardly as though he were talking about a low test score at school, Matt said, "They tell me I'm dying. . . . Yes . . . dying. I don't know. They first said in two weeks. Yes. I'm in shock. I knew it was coming, but . . . two weeks! Maybe it will be longer."

What Billy said on the other end of the line, I don't

know, but Matt's response was, "Yes, me too. I'll keep calling you. Okay. Good-bye."

When Matt told his Uncle David, Lydia's brother, that he was dying, David said, "Matt, that just blows me away. I don't know what to say."

Matt replied, "Oh, don't feel bad about that, Uncle David. No one does. No one knows what to say. It's all right."

And so he comforted us—those of us living with futures unthreatened and for whom dying is postponed for future consideration—he comforted us as he prepared for his final journey.

When you know you are dying, irrelevant things fall away. Matt's forthright way of facing his death helped put things in perspective for us. One day, Scott and Skip were so stressed that they grew angry with each other. I sat with Matt and lamented, "Matt, I am sorry that two people who love you and whom you love are having such a hard time getting along right now."

"Oh, don't worry about it, Granddad," Matt replied casually. "That's their problem."

Since I am prone to shoulder every problem around me as my personal responsibility, it helps to remember that there are times when benign neglect is in order. When you know that your remaining days on earth are certain to be intense and brief, carrying loads about which you can do nothing is a luxury you cannot afford. "That's their problem."

Throughout Matt's final months, I was amazed at the supportive attitudes expressed by unknown friends in unexpected places. For instance, the year before Lydia died, some hot air balloons launched regularly from a field near our house in Fort Worth. We often drove by as the balloons ascended. Matt and I talked of taking a balloon ride someday.

One day at a car wash, I struck up a conversation with a man who owned one of the hot air balloons Matt and I had admired from a distance. He was willing to take us up—for a price.

I telephoned Matt about it, and asked if he wanted to go for the ride of his life.

"No, Granddad. Mama and I have been talking about it. She wants to do it, too. I'll wait for her."

It was one of the many things that Lydia did not live long enough to do.

Even after Lydia died, Matt never forgot that hot air balloon ride he planned to take with his mama. I was unaware of Matt's mulling over this piece of unfinished business. He never shared it with me.

Then Matt's ending time began. Again, he brought up the subject of the balloon ride. Scott checked on the possibility, but he was told that Matt was too young and too small to meet the requirements for a balloon flight. The idea was dropped.

But the mother of one of Matt's fellow students at the Lakewood school decided to make a cause célèbre out of Matt's desire to go on a balloon flight. She contacted the president of a company that manufactures balloons in Albuquerque, New Mexico. He agreed to waive the rules and take Matt up in a balloon, if Matt could get to Albuquerque.

That was all that indefatigable mom needed to know.

She established a campaign to raise funds to send Matt to New Mexico. Announcing the idea at a parent-teacher's committee meeting, she stirred an interest. One of the women there attended midweek prayer services at the Church of Christ nearby. She told Matt's story there, and asked for prayer for the project. The pastor, who recently moved from a church in Richardson, was none other than Larry James, the man who had taken Matt into his church's summer day-care program when no one else would. Larry spoke of the family and his association with Matt.

In the congregation was Dr. Dan Cooper, a medical doctor whose child had died three years earlier. After the service, Dan told Larry that he would assume the financial obligation for getting Matt and his family to Albuquerque.

On a beautiful fall day, with the sun brightly shining and the winds whipping gently, Mary and Matt climbed into a festively colored balloon.

Through the help of numerous unexpected participants in our lives, Matt got his balloon ride. Balloons had always colored his life. Lydia had made them as symbolic as the dolphins she loved. Now, Matt drifted through the air in a basket, the spewing flame above him shooting hot air into the huge balloon, as he excitedly took in the sight of Albuquerque with the Sandia mountains in the background.

After returning to Dallas, Matt confessed, "Granddad, I really did it for Mama. She always wanted to do it. Now I can tell her about it when I see her."

Like his mother had done before him, Matt began meeting with friends and family members to say his last good-byes.

Scott and Matt went to the Lakewood school to meet with his sixth grade class. Matt talked to his schoolmates about dying and how it felt to know that life would soon be over. They took pictures of each other, dozens of them!

As far as Matt was concerned, the primary purpose of the visit was to get his picture taken with the girl on whom he had a secret crush for several years. Too shy to let her know about it, his illness blocked him from acknowledging his love. After the secret was out, his disease still kept him silent.

When people smile at puppy love, I remind them that no matter how silly it looks to others, it is real to the puppy. Children have profound emotions. Matt's had been bottled up inside him. In his privacy, he had not told me how deep and continuing were his feelings for this girl. I recalled that we had talked about her once, when she and Matt were in the fourth grade together. Then silence settled in. Matt carried his love unexpressed all that time.

The week following Valentine's Day in 1995, on a beautiful Texas winter day, the Lakewood Elementary School in Dallas conducted an outdoor ceremony to say a final good-bye to Matt, to celebrate his life, and to prepare his friends for his death. Several of Matt's schoolmates and teachers expressed what he had meant to them. To the music of "The Circle of Life" from the Disney movie *The Lion King*, the Lakewood students paraded around Matt, surrounding him with music, banners, and most of all, love.

Then it was Matt's turn. Standing shakily on an outdoor makeshift stage in the school's parking lot, Matt spoke to the students and teachers. In a voice that would have been barely audible had it not been for the help of a microphone, Matt said, "Thank you for all the support you have given me and my family over the past six years. It has meant so much to me, and them."

Many of Matt's friends and teachers were overcome by tears during the emotional ceremony. When it was over, everyone realized that death really is part of the circle of life.

*   *   *

That same week, following the circle of life ceremony, we had arranged for Matt to have his closing time with his great-grandmother, my eighty-five-year-old mother. Legally blind, but mentally alert, my mother lived comfortably in a home for the aging in Dallas. She kept up with world events through National Public Radio's news for the visually disadvantaged. In her senior years, my mother has not always been able to attend church services, but she listens to tapes of worship services several times each week. She is a good, godly woman.

Sadly, the specter of AIDS haunted even my mom. She grieved deeply as she dealt with the fears and thoughtlessness of her aged companions concerning AIDS. For several years while her family was devastated by the disease, she maintained absolute silence on the subject. After the family went public, she lived with some self-imposed isolation rather than endure the hurtful looks and comments from her peers. She left the church to which she had belonged because of the judgmentalism of some of its members. Soon, however, the silent sufferers around her began to share their pain over family members caught in the same devastation. As Matt's story came to light, the sympathy and understanding of friends began to surface. Now Mom is able to talk freely about the disease and its impact on her life and the lives of others.

Despite his fatigue, Matt realized the significance of a visit with my mother and initiated the idea. "Granddad, Papa says I need to say good-bye to Great Gran. Can you help me do it?"

I readily set it in motion.

Matt was too weak to shop for flowers or a gift for Great Gran, but he was determined that he take something with him. My mother collected elephant figurines for years. She never forgot the thrill when as a little girl she was lifted onto the trunk of a circus elephant for a ride around the ring! Then, there was the day in Detroit when Jumbo himself came to town. I was four years old at the time, and Mom took me to the P. T. Barnum and Bailey Circus so I wouldn't miss my chance to ride Jumbo.

I went to the store and walked down aisle after aisle looking for elephant figures. No elephants could be found. When I told Matt, he took it in stride. He had known so many disappointments in his twelve years that he had a well-used phrase of dismissal: "That's life."

We did the next best thing. We bought a colorful arrangement of artificial flowers.

"We don't want her to have to water them," Matt noted approvingly. We bought a beautiful card to go along with the bouquet, a card for someone who was a special friend. We were ready to go.

We arrived at the home after the doors were locked for the evening, and I knew we would have to wait outside for an attendant to come. Rather than having Matt expend the extra energy standing there, I retrieved the wheelchair from the trunk. Matt would have none of it. Shaky, unsteady, but determined, he said, "It'll be all right. I'll walk."

I put the wheelchair back in the trunk.

Matt's once-robust figure had withered. The marks of dying—gaunt skin tightly stretched across his cheekbones, eyes sunken in deep sockets—spoke eloquently and silently as he moved toward the doorway.

His Atlanta Braves baseball cap swallowed his head now, but Matt kept it on. The thinning of his lusterless hair had been one of his most sensitive concerns.

He had thought through what he would say, much as he had thought through his brief speech at the school that week. This time, however, he didn't keep it to himself. On the way, he said, "Granddad, this is what I am going to say to Great Gran, 'I came to tell you good-bye, because I may not ever see you again.' "

I didn't make any suggestions or alterations. This was Matt's moment with his great-grandmother.

We entered Great Gran's small apartment. We greeted one another and then we all sat on the sofa in her room. Matt got out the card and I placed the flowers on Great Gran's coffee table, as she quickly made room for them.

Matt informed Great Gran concerning the best aspect of the flowers. "You don't have to water them," he said. That was Matt, practical to the end.

Matt got right to the heart of his visit. He carefully chose his words and said, "Great Gran, I came to see you tonight because I may not ever see you again before I go to the Peaceful Place. I love you."

Great Gran rose to the occasion. "Thank you, Matthew. I know that, but you know I am going to see you again there. It may not be very long. You know I'm eighty-five years old. I love you."

They hugged. Matt winced. His skin had grown so tender that often it was painful to be touched. Lately, most family members allowed Matt to initiate any hugging. Great Gran had a hard time remembering that.

I have walked through dying with hundreds of families. But I have never seen an adult deal with the experience as courageously, calmly, and forthrightly as Matt. Twelve years of living with a disease that would ultimately take his life, the sorrowing over his mother's dying, the care his father had taken to inform him of the devastation of his body, and his faith that there is a Peaceful Place where his mother and brother awaited him combined to create in him an unusual maturity and purpose. He was dying with a great deal more courage, dignity, and grace than I showed in my grieving.

He wears his Atlanta Braves baseball cap nearly every waking moment of his final days. His sallow skin is taut across his hollow cheeks. He breathes in short, shallow breaths. That's how he looks in these final days, but that is not the image I will remember best.

I will always see a boisterous, busy little boy, shouting, "Come on Grandad; come and see!"

And now that energy is gone, victim of an illness he never surrendered to any day of his life. Matt has done everything possible to live his life to the fullest while holding the AIDS at bay. Now the battle is almost over.

The disease is winning. But Matt is not losing.

PART TWO

TWENTY

DEALING WITH THE WHYS

I COULDN'T SLEEP. That wasn't new. Stress does that to me. I popped awake at 2:30 A.M. while my body cried for rest. My thoughts scattered in every direction. I slipped out of bed, trying my best not to awaken Wanda, and tiptoed into the kitchen. I made a cup of coffee—decaffeinated, of course. I couldn't afford the extra jolt of caffeine in my system.

I walked out on the deck of our mountain home at Big Canoe. The moon rode high on a chariot of clouds. The cicadas sounded the pulsating rhythms of their mating songs. The mountain had taken on an eerie sort of beauty in the moonlit night. The gently swaying tree branches cast shadowy question marks that reflected the shadowy questions filling my mind.

From the earliest days of the secret, when I first heard the tragic news from Scott that our family was an AIDS family, I had consciously resisted the *why* questions—the Why-has-this-happened-to-us? type of queries—and instead focused my energies on the *how* questions, such as How are we going to get through this? Yet despite every effort to ignore the *why* and deal with the *how,* the why questions kept recurring.

As I peered into the moonlight that night on our deck, I thought of my boyhood days on my granddad's farm. I had worked in the cotton fields, pulling weeds by hand, up one row of cotton and down the next. As clean as I got a row, the next day, new green weeds had broken through the soil again. Similarly, try as I might to keep my mental fields clean, the weeds of *why* keep growing in my fertile mind:

Why has this disease happened to us?

Why have my children and grandchildren been part of this?

Why didn't God protect our family from this evil?

Why is there evil in the world, anyhow?

Why did God allow us to be born if he knew in advance that we would have to experience so much grief?

The *why* questions, like weeds in a cotton field, kept popping up.

I had my first authentic experience with grief when my dad died in the summer of 1973. I was delivering a paper to a study group at our national Baptist assembly grounds near Santa Fe, New Mexico. Scott was in high school, and I took him with me for some personal time in that beautiful place. The clear, crisp air of the foothills of the Sangre de Cristo range sharpened the view of rugged mountains, green scrubby trees, and red stone rocks. We stayed at a hotel in Santa Fe and drove each day to the assembly grounds just outside of town.

The day Dad died, I had driven to the assembly grounds to deliver my address. A telephone call came about an hour before the session. It was Luke Williams. I stood at the wall-mounted pay telephone in the lobby, as happy, excited people streamed by me. I expected Luke to inform me of some matter about the church where we served together. Instead, directly and briefly, Luke told me that my seventy-two-year-old father had died of a massive heart attack while working in his vegetable garden.

As Dad worked alongside his bride of many years, he sang "'Neath the Shade of the Old Apple Tree." Suddenly, he turned to Mom and said, "Doll, I have to go home now." With those words, he fell dead.

I gripped the telephone until my hand hurt. In a forcibly controlled voice, I asked Luke some questions, and he provided the information I needed to start making funeral arrangements and dealing with other details associated with the death of a loved one. I thanked Luke and hung up the telephone, oblivious to the people passing by on their way to hear me speak.

I postponed my grief by sheer willpower. I walked into the assembly, read the paper to the group, fielded their questions, and then announced my departure "because my father has just died."

As I drove back to Santa Fe to meet Scott and tell him what had happened, all my feelings tore loose. I knew Dad was a man of faith for whom death held no fear. I had no question about whether his life was satisfactory or his death victorious. I had no doubt my dad was already in heaven with Jesus. But that did not stop the pain that ripped my heart apart. That car became

my grieving chamber. I wept with a keening wail, ending in a shout of, "God, it hurts. It hurts!"

Every person who has ever grieved the loss of a loved
one and has grappled with the *why* questions has
known that awful feeling. Despite our faith, oftentimes,
life hurts.

The movie *Shadowlands* tells the story of how C. S.
Lewis came to terms with grief. This British man of
letters and Oxford don stumbled from atheism and ag-
nosticism into faith in Christ, where as he eloquently
described it he was "surprised by joy." I am one of
thousands Lewis has helped through his books, in
which he wrote so succinctly and insightfully about
faith and doubt and the search for truth.

Lewis was especially eloquent when he dealt with
pain and its meaning. For years, however, Lewis hid
behind his intellectualism as he examined the truths of
life, rarely risking his own emotional involvement.
Then C. S. Lewis fell in love. His relationship with an
American poet, Joy Davidman, developed first as
friend, then as protector for this strikingly honest
woman, and then as loving husband. When she died of
cancer, Lewis wrote his chronicle, *A Grief Observed*.

Shadowlands tells the story of how Lewis moved out
of the realm of theory and theology into authentic life
and love. The movie showed that describing death and
pain and suffering—even as articulately as Lewis did—
does not substitute for the emotional turmoil and inner
agony itself.

I was drawn to *Shadowlands* because I saw my reflection in the story. I have ministered to thousands of
grieving people. I have done so conscientiously and
truthfully, believing every word of the Scriptures I
pointed them to. I even played out the scenarios of my

own death, and how I hoped my family and I would face it. If it were possible to lessen the blow that grief deals, I should have been able to do it.

But when it came, it ripped me apart.

Each loss tore my heart open a little further—first Dad, then Bryan, Luke, and Lydia. Then as I watched Matt dying day by day, unable to prevent it from happening again. *Why?* The why questions became redundant and irrelevant.

It was not that I stopped asking them. But *why* questions are useless to those who simply struggle to make it through the day. Pondering and philosophizing over the *whys* of life are luxuries only those who have solved the issues of survival can afford. Persons stumbling across deserts, dehydrated, gasping for breath, staggering to make another step need no information on the ecological reasons for a sea evaporating and leaving sand in its stead. No information about the distance to the sun or the problems of ozone and radiation helps. Even the personal events leading up to having to cope with that place of blistering heat and jagged rocks are unimportant. The only things that matter are water, shade, and survival.

Yet the human mind will not stop questioning. It worries over a *why* dilemma like a dog with a thorn embedded in its paw. Attention may be momentarily diverted to more urgent matters, but the muted pain keeps throbbing for attention.

So the questions come calling when I least expect them. They come at night, when I am at the edge of consciousness, trying to sleep. Or in an unguarded moment as I hear a laughing child, the *why* questions leap across my path to challenge me. Why could it not be

Bryan laughing, or Matt, or Lydia? Why did they have to die so young?

If I had the answer to every why, I could chart every cause and effect in the universe. But doing so would not add a thing to the struggle to survive. When you grapple with life itself, the issue is how to manage it. How do you keep grief from suffocating you? How do you deal with pain that cuts through your inner psyche like a dull and jagged knife? How do you handle the stress of constantly second-guessing your every action to determine whether you are helping or hurting those you love most? How do you deal with feelings of rejection, fear, and shame—especially when you have done nothing to justify such responses?

Anyone who has had to grapple with the *why* questions that result from life's senseless tragedies knows those feelings.

To adequately address the *whys*, we must start with the pain and perplexity of God. It is not enough to start with our own pain. We feel it deeply; we may even be overwhelmed by it, but we can't understand it if we simply concern ourselves with our own lives.

We live in a universe created by God out of some driving, mysterious, loving impulse. He created us to have fellowship with him. Imagine, then, God's pain, when mankind rebelled against him in the Garden of Eden, and has continued to do so throughout history. Since God is intimately concerned with and involved with everything in his world, the pain to which he made himself vulnerable is beyond our comprehension.

Why did he do that? Why didn't he create some strategy to avoid grief in our world? Better still, why not maintain a perfect world, with no flawed layers of moving rock plates deep within the earth, out of which earthquakes can shatter the surface; no floods sweeping across the land most likely to provide food for the world; or simply no hunger, thirst, pain, or sickness? Furthermore, why didn't God eliminate any possibility of rebellion by those whose love he desired? He certainly had the power to do that. But some things cannot be attained by power alone.

To gain a loving response from his people, he had to risk rejection and a hateful response. To gain people in harmony with his purpose, he had to risk those who have purposes of their own that do not include him. Therefore, we live in a twisted world where disease and death take innocent lives. We live in a world where, sadly, people often do great damage in their ignorance and fear. Ignorance often creates fear, and fear paralyzes love. And God hurts, too.

I am moved by the story of the bitter man who cried out, "Where was God? Where was God when my boy died?"

The response was, "I guess he was crying, too, just like he did when his Boy died."

After all, God did not immunize himself or his own son from pain, suffering, and grief. Even Jesus had to deal with the ultimate *why* question. Think of the cry of Jesus on the cross in the midst of his agony as he appealed to his heavenly Father, "Why have you forsaken me?"

The unspoken answer to that question is, "Because I couldn't do it any other way." God could not save us any other way.

At that point, the heart of God was vulnerable and hurting because, like a loving father, he felt the pain and suffering his children experienced. God has lived with that pain. And oftentimes, that is where his love comes to touch us. The One who loved, cared, and suffered like that is the God I serve. He loves and cares and suffers over me.

Still, I now live with mystery. The mystery is that he enters into my suffering with me. Because he is in the midst of my pain, there is strength. There is assurance that life is not always going to be this way, that ultimately, God will bring us back to himself. Therefore, I can be assured of the victory, and can claim pieces of it right now.

My victories come in small, hour-by-hour pieces. I don't have the victory of the constantly tranquil; my victories come in the midst of tumult. But the assurances come in wonderful ways produced by God's mystery. Sometimes they come through impressions in my heart and mind. Sometimes they come as I read the Bible; I will run across a passage that speaks especially to me such as, "My help comes from the Lord." God's Word speaks to me again and again about the strength that God gives. He is the Rock of salvation.

In the midst of my family's struggle with AIDS, a dear friend of mine, Pastor Bruce McIver, asked me, "How on earth do you hold up?"

My answer may have surprised him. I said, "I've stopped asking God for victory, and started asking him for strength."

Because of what my family has experienced, friends sometimes refer to me as a modern-day Job, alluding to the Old Testament character known for his undeserved suffering. Although I appreciate my friends' sentiments, I really do not care to inherit that dubious distinction. Job was, after all, a bit of a whiner. He complained and lamented constantly about his experiences.

Not that he did not have reason to complain. He was

a righteous man. If life was going to work out well for someone, Job certainly qualified. But after achieving great success in the world, Job lost everything he had —possessions, family, health, respect of his colleagues, even the support of his wife who urged Job to give up and simply curse God and die.

But Job refused to give up. He refused to speak evil against God. In the face of horrible personal tragedies, Job continued to trust God.

Interestingly, Job's knowledge of the Lord was much more limited than ours. Job had only sparse information concerning the way God works in people's lives. He responded to a God about whom he knew little—only a vague revelation that there was an all-powerful, all-knowing Creator. We, on the other hand, have centuries of God's self-disclosure through his Word, through the example of Jesus Christ, and through the life experiences of those who have come to know God intimately.

Yet we, too, must learn the lesson God impressed upon Job. God showed him that Job was not the center of the universe; *God* was the center of Job's universe. God never answered Job's many *why* questions; God simply refocused Job's attention on the *who* and the *how* questions. Who is in charge here? and How are you going to respond? Though decimated in many ways, Job hung on by faith, no matter what the cost. Through all of his troubles, Job's most famous cry was, "Though he slay me, yet will I hope in him" (Job 13:15). If that seems foolish, that's the kind of fool I want to be.

Job's reward? He ultimately caught a glimpse of God. As Job's triumphant moment of understanding came, limited though it was, he could say to God, "Now my eyes have seen you" (Job 42:5). It is almost anticlimactic when God then restored Job's health and possessions, and gave him more family members.

I am convinced that grief comes to us as well, not to destroy us, but to draw us closer to God. Not a result of intelligence, good works, or any other self-righteousness, this closeness comes only by trusting him, no matter what. The issue turns out to be, then, not how to avoid pain or blame God for it, but what we are to learn about the God who shares it with us.

Yet the myth persists that God owes us protection. Our sense of justice is assailed by the fact that evil acts do not always bring evil results and good acts do not always bring good results. There are a thousand parables about it. "Good seed produces good harvest." "Crime doesn't pay." Why, then, do bad things happen to good people? Why does God not provide protection and immunization to the people who follow him?

Nobody can say for certain, but it is probable that God chose not to operate that way so we would love *him,* rather than simply loving the comfort he can provide. What if God drew a magic circle around our lives? Consider this imaginary deal: Love and obey God, and you are in the circle of his love. No evil can reach you. You are guarded against pain. Outside the circle, you are exposed to the worst that life can throw at you—tragedies, rip-offs, selfishness, debilitating diseases, and death.

Who wouldn't want to get into that magic circle? But would we love God, or his magic circle? Most of us would climb into the circle to avoid pain and discomfort, not to express our love to God.

That's why there are no magic circles when you walk with Christ. Christians are not immune to the tragedies of life. They experience the best and worst life has to offer. The difference between Christians and unbelievers is that Christians believe in a God who not only has experienced our pain, but chooses to walk with us through our pain. No matter what strikes our lives, Jesus says, "I am with you."

With that in mind, perhaps rather than ask Why us? we should ask Why not us? Is not God's strength adequate to carry us through the same trials our fellow human beings encounter? What good is a gospel that works only when the sun shines and life is easy? Our emotional and spiritual muscles develop when they are stretched to the breaking point. Athletes work at stretching their physical muscles because they know that strength comes through struggle. In the midst of our struggle, all we can think about is survival. But the goal for the Christian is not simply survival. It is a peace that passes understanding. It is to thrive. It is to know joy.

The writer of Hebrews attributes this quality to Jesus, "Who for the joy set before him endured the cross, scorning its shame, and sat down at the right hand of the throne of God" (Heb. 12:2). Should not those of us who follow him do likewise?

Over and over again I hear, "You seem to get more than your share of suffering." I wrote a friend recently when I learned he was going through some hard times. He called me to say, "When I got your letter, I felt I was hearing from Job, 'I'm sorry about your bad cold and I hope it's better!'"

I appreciated his call, but like many of us, he had a misconception of the way we categorize our suffering. Somehow we have conceived of pain and suffering in quantitative terms. The idea is that everybody has a share. If you have a lot of it, you have more than should be demanded of you. If you have less than your share, you are lucky. We tend to think, *It could be worse. Look at what is happening to that person.* But pain, especially the emotional pain of tragic losses in our lives, is not a measured commodity to be placed on a scale, weighed, and assigned a numerical equivalent.

People sometimes say to me, "Compared to the pain you and your family have experienced, my pain is nothing." They almost feel guilty for feeling discouraged or depressed. When I encounter such a person, I gently explain that comparing pain is inappropriate, and more importantly, irrelevant. The fact is each of us is hurting about as much as we can bear. Regardless of how much or how little pain we must endure, our sufferings are real. Our thresholds of pain may differ. The shape of our pain is infinitely varied. But the size of it is our own capacity. No one has room for any more pain.

Life does not come out even. The ancients were right when they depicted justice as a blindfolded woman holding scales in her hand. The day of true justice will not come until that day promised in the Bible when Christ returns to reign, when no mystery remains and perfect justice is achieved. To believe that and to expect it is an act of faith. In the meantime, life is not fair. The innocent suffer with the guilty, and sometimes because of the guilty. The rain falls on the righteous and the unrighteous. We may be offended by that, but it is true.

I hear someone say, "You don't deserve to hurt like this."

I want to reply, Who does?

Suffering is no less painful for the guilty than it is for the innocent. We act as if the fact that one has contributed to his own dilemma absolves us of our responsibility to care about his agony.

Jesus did not regard people like that. He held no inquisitions with women taken in the act of adultery, thieves dying beside him on the cross, or greedy men straining to see him in the crowd. He simply forgave. He never probed for probable causes of wasted bodies with crooked limbs, lepers with flesh falling off their bones, or people with eyes unable to see the sunlight. Jesus simply healed.

Let's admit it, overeating causes obesity, which can lead to a heart attack; smoking causes lung cancer; intoxication causes bodies to be smashed in automobile collisions; sexual misbehavior creates an environment in which a virus can destroy immune systems. But do we refuse to care about the dying because they deserve to endure the consequences of their deeds? Can a shrugged shoulder, a raised eyebrow, and a turned head become our response because "they brought it on themselves"?

Jesus knew all the sordid intricacies of sinners' lives, but he did not heap more abuse upon them. He started with them in their sinful situations and used their circumstances to show them who he was, and what he wanted to do in their lives. He came to seek and save those who were lost. He said from the beginning of his ministry that his purpose was to "preach the gospel to the poor . . . to heal the brokenhearted, to preach deliverance to the captives, and recovering of sight to the blind, to set at liberty them that are bruised, to preach the acceptable year of the Lord" (Luke 4:18-19, KJV).

Maybe I am more similar to Job than I know, for God never answered my *why* questions. Since the issue of who is in charge of my life was settled long ago, God focused my attention on the *how*—How can we deal with this?

He helped me realize that the authentic question about AIDS is not How did you get it? It is How do you get through it?

Indeed, every effort must be made to prevent the disease. We now know enough to help people avoid it. Nevertheless, no medical cure exists for AIDS. Nor is it possible for people to be immunized against it. We *can,* however, encourage sexual behavior patterns that will diminish it—and we must.

For my family, the issue is no longer *why us?* It is How can we help others avoid the suffering that has come to us?

TWENTY-ONE

WHEN GOD SAYS NO

A MYSTERIOUS RELATIONSHIP exists between prayer and healing. That God can heal is obvious. The Bible is replete with instances in which God brought about physical as well as emotional and spiritual healings. Often the eye of faith discerns a correlation between prayer and healing. No disease seems to be beyond the reach of these incidents. People with cancer, heart problems, and other complex diseases seem to postpone death by their faith and the intercessory prayers of others.

Yet the results of such prayers are unpredictable.

When the telephone call came to tell us of the deadly blood transfusions given to my family members, I im-

mediately entered into desperate prayer. I laid out our
need again and again to the Father. In an eager yearning to avoid the facts, I prayed that somehow they
might not be true. That stage did not last long. It became obvious that there was no mistake in the diagnosis—our family had AIDS.

I quickly moved into the next phase, in which by
sheer faith, I asked God to intervene and heal my family members. He chose not to do so. I can only specu-
late why he chose not to return my family to good
health.

The Father and I have had a long relationship. Prayer
has played a pivotal part in my life. I have been nurtured in the art of seeing God's hand at work in the
smallest details of life. A sense of his immediacy, his
present-tense activity, permeated my parental home
and my early life. Not only did we pray for food in
those early mission-starting days in the inner city of
Dallas, we prayed about everything.

I have kept a journal over the years, a chronicle of
my spiritual journey. In it I have written insights I have
discovered, as well as prayer requests and answers to
prayer. Recently, I reviewed some of the entries. To my
delight, I found petition after petition answered. Some
of them were answered years after I asked. Some of
them still await a specific response from God.

Because prayer is central to my relationship with the
Father, it was disconcerting when my prayers were not
answered as I expected. I prayed, as did others, for
Bryan to live. He died. I prayed for Luke to live, but he
died, too. I prayed for Lydia to live. She died. What
was wrong? Why were my prayers so ineffective?
God said no.

I faced some hard questions: What do we do when God turns down our requests? How do we deal with unanswered prayers?

It is important to understand that God always answers prayer. No prayer goes unnoticed by the one who "numbers the hairs of your head." Neither is any prayer ignored. Sometimes God answers yes. Against great odds, the request fits into the pattern of his plan. He answers. Things happen. These are the times best remembered. They are the prayer experiences we speak of frequently to friends and family. They are the answers to prayer that we bear witness to at church.

Although God is not limited to human resources and ingenuity, he often uses processes he has already built into his creation to bring about the answer. During our seminary days, Wanda's tuition was due at the university. It was $158, but it might as well have been a million. We didn't have it. We prayed. I prayed fervently, since my new bride had left the security of a well-to-do family for a precarious financial future with me in the ministry. But just in time, a check arrived in the mail— a gift of $160. We had two dollars to spare!

That moment became symbolic of my later experiences of trusting God to provide millions of dollars for tasks he wanted to be done in his world. And he never let me down. Of course, I am not alone in seeing such tangible answers to prayer. The cumulative testimony of believers through the centuries assures us that God can and often does say yes to our prayers.

At other times, God's answer to our prayer is wait. This may be the toughest answer we can hear. We constantly contend with time and with our sense of urgency. Our greatest struggle with prayer is that we want answers *now*. Impatience characterizes me. Yet what I perceive as unanswered prayer often has proved to be merely wait-on-the-Lord time. As I go through my prayer journals, I find ample testimony to that truth. One of the most memorable incidents concerned our oldest son, Michael, who is diagnosed schizophrenic, and has had to deal with a fragmented personality since early childhood.

I should have recognized it when the green house disappeared.

When Michael was in third grade, we lived about two blocks from the elementary school he attended. When I arrived home from the church one afternoon, Michael came to me to say, "Daddy, the green house has disappeared and the little boy I played with there is gone, too."

I replied, "What green house, Mike?"

"The one that was on the corner about three blocks from school. It's gone. It's just not there anymore."

I said, "Now, Mike, houses don't just disappear. Maybe they have hauled it off. Do you remember seeing those big trucks on the highway, carrying houses from one place to another? Maybe they've moved the house."

"No, Daddy, it's just gone."

I decided he had gotten mixed up about which corner the green house was on, so I said, "Come get in the car. Maybe you're confused about where the house is. How far is it from the school?"

"About three blocks." He was sure. We drove around the neighborhood, up and down every street within five blocks of the school—no green house. I could not even remember a green house.

Finally I said, "Mike, sometimes we have really vivid dreams, dreams that seem so real we think they happen. Maybe you were dreaming of a little boy and a green house and now you are awake."

"No, Daddy. It was there. But now it's gone."

The incident passed. Forgotten for years, it came up again in Mike's young adulthood. Wanda and I had gone through ordeal after ordeal with him. Psychologists at school simply thought he was being pressed too hard by our expectations that he produce academically. We didn't agree, but followed their advice and lowered our expectations.

Michael began to develop aberrant behavior. We walked with him through all kinds of struggles, including stints in mental hospitals, special schools, and substance-abuse treatment programs. In a San Antonio psychiatric hospital one day, Mike said, "Dad, do you remember the green house that disappeared? I knew then that I was not normal. That hallucination was so real I still remember it." I remembered it, too. I will never forget it.

Michael struggled from hospital to hospital over the years and still was nonfunctioning, until finally I was worn out with hoping. My prayers for Michael's healing seemed to go nowhere. Eventually, I stopped praying for him to be healed. I despaired at his ever functioning beyond his paranoia and separation from reality.

My dad, however, refused to give up praying for Mike.

Not long before Dad died, he became the pastor-director of the Baptist historical center at Independence, Texas. At the height of my anxiety over Michael, I paid my parents a visit, and Mike's illness quickly surfaced in our conversation.

Dad said, "Son, I have been praying for Michael,

and I have received assurance that Michael will be well. He is going to be able to function."

"Dad," I replied, "I simply can't believe that. We've tried everything. I've prayed until I am worn out. I can't muster that hope. But I do believe in your faith. I have watched your faith. I have faith in your faith. I can't ask God to heal Michael anymore, but you can. I'll have to leave it like that."

My dad died before Michael could find any answers to his medical problems. Shortly after Dad's death, we found a medication that allows Michael to function normally. He does so today. The condition did not disappear but it is under control. He can work. He has a family. He has a lovely little daughter, Diana, our only other grandchild, who attends elementary school in San Antonio. Michael is a loving and caring human being. Most of all, he loves God.

Dad's prayers were answered. The waiting was worth it. In my prayer journals, next to Michael's name, the word *Answered* is scrawled numerous times, not because of my prayers, but because of Dad's prayers. But it took time for the answers to come. God had said wait.

God's most mystifying answer to prayer is *no*. That answer shouldn't surprise those of us who are parents. We say no to our children when their requests are unreasonable or dangerous. Yet we often allow a negative response from God to undercut our confidence in prayer.

We do so because we see prayer simply as asking and receiving. We know that God is the keeper of good things. We want to believe that if we please him and pray believing, he will open the storehouse and give us anything we want.

But real prayer far transcends a give-and-get mentality. It is a means of putting us in harmony with God. Knowing God as friend becomes paramount. We want to fellowship with him. We shift from loving God for what we can get out of him to simply wanting to be in his presence.

Somewhere along the way, Matthew got the idea that his granddad was rich. Maybe it was because we lavished him with travel and other experiences. When he was eight, money became important to him. He had made the connection. He lived in a frugal household because of all the financial burdens his parents carried. His comfortable yet meager home suddenly seemed different from those of his schoolmates and neighbors.

One day we chatted during a just-us-guys time. We had been to a park and a movie that day. We ate popcorn during the movie, and now decided that a milk shake was in order. As we enjoyed our shakes, Matt mused aloud, "Granddad, do you know what I would like to have? I'd like to have your bank account."

"No, Matt," I answered, to his surprise. Matt was not accustomed to me saying no to him about many things. "That would be very bad for us," I continued. "Though my bank account isn't nearly as big as you think it is, that still would be very bad for us. You see, that would mean you don't love me, you just love my bank account. If we love each other, each of us has what the other has. If you just love what the other guy has, it means you are not loving at all."

Matt pondered a while and said, "Oh! Good point!"

Similarly, when God says no, he guards against our loving what he provides rather than loving the One who provides it. Yet in some religious circles there is an energetic call for faith that says that if you believe strongly enough, all things are possible. That simplistic call has created guilt in many sincere people to whom God has said no. It presupposes that God's role in my life is to make sure that I am happy, wealthy, healthy, and successful. In its crassest form, this doctrine is called name-it-and-claim-it or believe-it-and-receive-it faith.

Frankly, it frustrated our family when well-intentioned, sincere people assured us that they were claiming Matt's healing. They cited instances of immediate healings from all kinds of diseases. The implication was that we ought to expect a miracle. Since I believe in miracles, the conversations sometimes were awkward.

I believe that God heals to fulfill some need in his kingdom. More must come from that act than simply making the person well. His healings usually consist of speeding up, in unusual ways, the healing processes he has built into our natures. On the other hand, if he chooses to heal with a touch of his hand, who am I to argue with that?

However God chooses to heal, it is always tied to his choice and purpose, not simply our demands, or even our temporary well-being. As difficult as it may be to believe, sometimes God's purposes are fulfilled more powerfully by not healing immediately. Sometimes his purposes are best served by the eternal healing that comes with death. That is what I have come to believe about the circumstances through which my family has lived, and died.

There is an authentic faith that does not expect a miracle. My faith is never surprised by miracles. I believe in them. I think they are wonders from our point of view. If we had an eternal point of view, we would see them as a part of God's divine pattern and intention. They are real. Explaining them or describing possible reasons for their occurrence does not remove the reality of their happening.

There is, however, a faith just as authentic and real that does not require a miracle. It sees all of life as a miracle, every breath, every scene of God's creation, every possibility of mind and thought. It sees God's promises as always conditional, not simply on my attitude but also on his purposes.

The Bible says we are to pray in Jesus' name. That is not simply a formula for closing a public pronouncement. It is a condition of prayer. It means that we want our prayer to be consistent with what Jesus would pray. The request must bear the scrutiny of whether it authenticates the claims of God or moves forward the purpose of God. If it is essential for that, nothing can prevent it happening. If it is not essential for that, nothing can make it happen.

If God was obligated to perform by the formulas of our faith and the intensity of our prayers, ultimate control would be in the hands of those who possess the formula. I would control God. He would have to do my will, rather than the other way around.

Thankfully, God is bigger than that. His purposes are beyond my understanding. Real faith is loving him, not for his storehouse of power, not for his solutions to our struggles, but for himself. Faith that can take it when God says no adds steel to resolve, peace to the soul, sensitivity to the suffering of a hurting world, and absolute confidence that God ultimately will make all things right.

I would have been ecstatic if God had healed my family members of AIDS. I have no doubt that we would have used the experience for his glory. But for reasons known only to himself, God chose not to provide an instantaneous miracle of healing. Our responsibility now is to use that experience, as well, for his glory.

TWENTY-TWO

THE CHURCH'S GREATEST CHALLENGE

THE AIDS EPIDEMIC provides the Church of Jesus Christ with an opportunity to express loving compassion. AIDS is a new, different sort of disease. Consequently, dealing with people who have been affected by the disease may well be the greatest challenge our modern-day churches have. Ironically, AIDS may also force many contemporary churches to examine their motives for existence, to rediscover their mission in the world, and to reconnect with the Power to get that mission accomplished.

I am concerned about the increasing impotence of institutions of religion in our secularized society. Families of God need to be freed from the captivity of their culture. They need vitality restored to their faith. Despite a stirring of interest in things of the Spirit, our church institutions are floundering, feuding, and failing.

The church is at its best when it escapes the captivity of its culture, and strips down to the basic task of loving, serving, and sharing the mystery of God's presence with hurting people. I visited with Mother Teresa when she came to my city. She invited me to Calcutta to see her people at work, and Wanda and I decided to go.

When we arrived in Calcutta, the scene was overpowering. The stench of the streets filled with dying people combined with the misery and filth all around us. I was profoundly impressed with Mother Teresa's houses for the dying, located in a culture in which the dead were hauled away from the streets every morning.

I watched the eagerness of orphaned children as they reached out for affection. I saw the mentally retarded lovingly cared for. But most of all, I saw the smiles, the unstinting good humor, the constant and unfeigned cheerfulness of the women who worked with Mother Teresa. They were happily engaged in loving and touching the least, the last, the lonely. They took literally the idea that as they served others, they served their Lord. Compassion had brought a vitality to their lives.

I could not help contrasting the loving expressions on the faces of people working in the stench and squalor of Calcutta with the artificial smiles of people I had seen in worship throughout my lifetime as a career church leader. As people in our comfortable sanctuaries turn to their neighbors at the appointed time in the service to smile and shake hands, they often parrot without feeling the words the worship leader has given them.

I often encouraged congregations to express their

openness to each other by their actions. It bothered me that the same handshaking people ignored each other outside of church, but I shrugged off their unconcern as merely human nature.

My experience in Calcutta changed all that, as did my disillusionment with our churches in my family's time of crisis with AIDS. I now find myself in the awkward position of trying to define and defend the role of churches in a society that rewards congregations more for successful building programs than for rescuing the dying. Sadly, there is no defense, and I know it. I wince with pain every time my son Scott, wounded by his rejection by the churches, says, "Dad, it's just a business like any other business. AIDS scares people away. Churches do what pleases the most customers."

In years past, I would have disagreed with Scott. No longer.

I'm having what I call a "lover's quarrel" with the church—not merely Baptist churches, but all churches that claim to represent Jesus Christ. I suffer the hurt, pain, and disillusionment of a disappointed lover. My life has been intertwined with the life of churches. I yearn for them to fulfill their high calling of God. I love the church. God gave his only Son for it, and my favorite term for the church is still the "family of faith." But I lament that, like many families, the family of faith is not functioning as it was intended by its Founder.

I have watched a creeping paralysis develop in many groups of believers who began with the best of intentions. Most Christian churches begin with the goal of meeting the needs of people with the spiritual message and ministry they communicate. Because such a church will inevitably become a place where battered, broken, bruised people congregate, the church soon begins to grow. With size and success comes the need for bigger buildings, larger budgets, and specialized institutions, all ostensibly for the purpose of more effective ministry to hurting people. Gradually, leadership roles are redefined and pastors and spiritual leaders find themselves becoming managers rather than ministers.

Good managers look for models of success and analyze the elements of success. A demand rises for quantitative goals since things that cannot be measured are difficult to duplicate. Our society has found ways to study itself with a high degree of accuracy. Nowadays, those same tools are used by religious institutions, as well.

Studying demographics and secular success models is not necessarily wrong. Unfortunately, the church has allowed the science of people-gathering to reach new heights, while oftentimes forgetting the main reason for gathering them. We have gotten caught up in a church growth movement that reflects what people are looking for—homogenous, comfortable, and secure surroundings in which emotional needs and family needs are met. As we meet these felt needs, and see large numbers of people responding, we interpret that response as the mark of God's blessing, when in fact, God may have little to do with it.

The spiraling costs of keeping everybody in the church comfortable and happy creates enormous financial pressure on churches. The competition is severe; the debt on the church building is high; we cannot afford to lose anyone; we cannot bear inner controversy, so we avoid issues that make us uncomfortable. One of those issues today is AIDS, but it is not the only social issue many modern churches avoid.

I cannot forget the conversation I had with a pastor of one of the largest evangelical churches in the nation. He recounted the opinion surveys about growing churches and what makes them attractive to the younger crowd he was trying to enlist. He said, "I hate to say it, but it's true. They don't like wheelchairs in the sanctuary. It just makes them feel uncomfortable." The church he pastors has no wheelchairs. I wondered if that pastor began his ministry with that attitude. If the passion for God drove him, I am sure he did not. I know I did not.

Most churches, pastors, and individual Christians begin their work for God with a spiritual motivation that goes somewhat like this:

The love of God reaching out to every person in need is one of the high callings of God in Christ Jesus. People are in trouble. They are wandering around without an answer. They are headed for eternity without hope. They are twisted and need to be brought into harmony. The healing touch of Christ can make the difference. I need to help bring that healing touch, motivated by Christ's love, to people who are hopeless, helpless, and hurting.

But as the years go by and successes or failures pile up, we lose our enthusiasm for helping hurting people. Instead we live by the numbers. Crowds are counted. And the effectiveness of our work for God is gauged by the number of notches we have been able to add to our "spiritual six-guns."

A powerful scene in the film *Brother Sun, Sister Moon* depicts that plight. This classic movie centers on the life of St. Francis of Assisi, a warrior who became a barefoot priest. In a vision, Francis heard the command of God, "Build my church." This involved not simply laying rocks, but changing attitudes.

The common people followed Francis in droves. He was so popular, the Vatican became disturbed about the movement and worried whether it was subversive, since it attracted so many of the homeless and restless of society. Francis was ordered to go to Rome to give an account of his teachings and to submit to a check of his orthodoxy.

As Francis made his way to Rome, the crowds following him became immense. Finally, Francis arrived in Rome and stood before the Pope.

In the movie, the encounter takes place in an ornate building with high marble steps. The steps are lined with church leaders dressed in gold-trimmed robes and headgear. The Pope sits on a throne at the top of the stairs, also in full regalia. The movie's director spared no pains in showing the sterility of the atmosphere.

In comes Francis, barefoot, joy-filled, and serene. As Francis kneels, to everyone's surprise, the Pope stands, and walks slowly down the steps. He pulls Francis up from his kneeling position. The Pope looks long into Francis's face and says in a husky whisper, "Once, long ago . . . when I first started . . . I thought . . . I wanted to . . ." His voice breaks, and the Pope kneels and kisses the young monk's feet.

One cynical advisor whispers to another, "The old man's a political genius. He'll have all the poor rabble eating out of his hand now." But the cryptic religious strategist missed the point. What really happened was that a man with a dream now lost, a vision unfulfilled, had suddenly remembered what it was he started out to do long ago.

In many ways, that's where our churches are today. We have long forgotten what it was we set out to do—to reach the world with Jesus' message of love, and his healing touch through us.

When AIDS hit our family, I was sure the church would respond better than it did, not because it was our family that was afflicted, but because it could have

been anybody's family. I believed that given the information and insight, inspired by a leader with vision, the
local church would rise above being an institution and
become a family. Families function with compassion as
well as confrontation. Families care for each other.
Families are accepting and open. I forgot that families
can also become dysfunctional. They can lose their direction. They can suffer from broken communication.
They can center on what they look like instead of who
they are.

When Scott was jobless and broken, several individuals
in churches and within our denomination reached out
to him. Some assisted with finances to underwrite his
salary. The Wilshire Baptist Church in Dallas, and its
pastor Bruce McIver, provided crucial assistance. Scott
and Lydia's house in Dallas could not have been purchased without help from volunteers from that church.
Some of those volunteers cleaned up the house and
made repairs. Others offered their presence or recreational activities.

The real issue, however, for Scott and Lydia, turned
out to be more than food, clothing, and shelter. It was
the disappointment they felt when the system they had
worked so hard to perpetuate failed to come through
for them. They had spent their time and energy enlist-
ing families in Christian activity. They had led the way
in taking care of church nurseries, visiting in homes to
bring ministry to people, and reaching out to anyone
who needed help. But when they needed help, the
church as an institution was not there for them. Christian individuals helped, but the organized church was
unwilling to risk reaching out to Scott and Lydia. After
ministering to multitudes of others, there was no place
where they and their child could go for nurture and

worship. The church's door slammed in their faces, and it left an indelible mark on my family.

While Matt still was able to attend school, I had lunch one day with him and some new friends. I listened intently as Matt described his experience with churches to his dining companions. Referring to an incident at church, Matt nonchalantly said, "That was before they kicked us out."

I have never heard sadder words.

Although damaged by the church at a young age, Matt at least had a loving, supportive Christian family to help point him toward the Peaceful Place. Others who have AIDS do not have anyone to love them and to tell them of God's love. Reaching these people and their families with the message of hope and salvation is the church's greatest challenge.

If we hope to reach out to them, we must hurry. Everyone with AIDS is dying; we must reach them before it is too late. But how?

TWENTY-THREE

WHAT CAN
WE DO?

DESPITE OUR CULTURE's heightened awareness of and increased sensitivity to people with HIV and AIDS, many victims and their families still fear rejection. One thing that motivated me to write this book was a 1994 telephone call from a public health worker in the northern part of my birthplace state, Arkansas.

At the time, I had not made any AIDS awareness speeches, written any books or articles, or done much of anything to increase AIDS awareness. My family had gone public with our secret over two years earlier, but by 1994 my emotions were nearly raw. I felt as though all my nerves were exposed, and somebody scraped them with a metal probe. Besides that, Matt's condition had begun to deteriorate, and each day brought new wounds too painful to talk about.

Then came that telephone call.

The health worker was looking for a videotape of the NBC *Dateline* program that aired two years earlier. On it, she had seen Scott and Matt interviewed, and heard for the first time the story of the church's refusal to receive them. The woman sounded desperate.

"I'm looking for the tape," she explained, "because there are people in this area with AIDS who are being kicked out of their churches today!"

She explained that she wanted to use the tape to help some of the families with AIDS who had been asked to leave their churches.

"I want to show them that they are not the only ones," she said sadly.

We talked further, and I promised the woman that I would secure a copy of the program for her. After I hung up the telephone, I sat in my office chair and sighed deeply. *Eight years,* I thought. *Eight years have gone by since we began this ordeal and still people are being kicked out of churches because of ignorance and fear of AIDS.* I was deeply disturbed that despite all the knowledge we had gained about AIDS, this could still be happening.

I thought, *If we haven't made any more progress than that, I ought to be doing something to help.* I began asking God what he wanted me to do.

Two days later, I received another telephone call, this one from television evangelist James Robison. Jim and I have known each other for years, and have agreed to disagree on many theological points. We are brothers in Christ, and we love each other, even though we differ on many issues.

I was surprised to hear his voice on the phone.

"Where have you been?" Jim joked. "I've been looking for you. I lost contact with you after you moved from Texas. I've wanted to contact you ever since the news about your family came out," Jim said, "and now seems to be the right time."

Jim was speaking more than he knew.

"I want you to consider letting me interview you on our television program. You know I believe in healing, but I want you to come and tell our audience about your experience with your family."

"Jim, I am not sure I can do that," I replied. "I have not done anything like that since this thing began. I will have to pray about it. I will call you back."

I thought about those folks in the churches of Arkansas, many of whom were fond of James Robison. I realized that I had asked God what he wanted me to do, and now here was an opportunity to speak directly to an audience that probably would not accept much information about AIDS from another source, but might if they heard it on James Robison's television program. I prayed about the opportunity and then called James. I told him I would come.

James Robison and I did three programs—on AIDS, on the problem of evil in our world, and on whether God is obligated to heal because we ask him to do so. The response to the programs was overwhelming. I received calls for more information about our story and what Christians could do in their churches to help minister to victims of AIDS.

From that point on, I knew I could be silent no longer. I must speak out. I must do something to help educate people about AIDS. Even more importantly, I had to help our churches find ways to minister to the ever-increasing HIV population around us.

Soon, someone from the T. B. Maston Foundation

called me and asked, "Would you speak at our annual meeting and tell your family's story?"

Again I responded by saying, "I have not done anything like that yet, but I'll pray about it, and get back to you."

T. B. Maston, the foundation's namesake, was this century's best-known Baptist ethicist, a man whose Christ-centered probing of the church's responsibility to be involved in social issues pricked the consciences of many Christians. Undoubtedly, Maston inspired innumerable social-action programs undertaken by Christians of all denominations.

I prayed about the opportunity and felt that I should speak to this group about AIDS. My presentation at that meeting was filmed and used as the Texas Baptist Christian Life Commission joined the foundation in helping produce a videotape entitled *Echoes from the Valley, a Beginning of an AIDS Ministry.* The Women's Missionary Union of the Southern Baptist Convention is using this tape as a tool for their AIDS awareness emphasis.

The tape included a segment with Matt's pediatrician, Dr. Janet Squires, answering questions most Sunday school and children's ministry personnel have about AIDS and what precautions are necessary to minister to AIDS children and their families. A third segment of the tape is a panel discussion by three people who worked with AIDS ministries in churches, one of whom was Larry James, the pastor who made a place for Matt in his church's day-care program. The Women's Missionary Union was so concerned that the information be distributed, they gave, free of charge, a videotape and workbook to key leaders desiring to establish an AIDS ministry.

* * *

Times are changing, and there are encouraging signs that the church is awakening to the AIDS challenge. In each of the congregations that refused to allow Matt to attend their Sunday schools, infectious-disease policies have now been established. A positive effort now is made to minister to AIDS children. In several churches in the Dallas-Fort Worth area, AIDS support groups have been formed.

Charles Wade, pastor of the First Baptist Church of Arlington, Texas, related to me that scores of churches from all over the nation have contacted the church he pastors to secure copies of their action plans for setting up an AIDS ministry. Various religious groups have created study materials to assist local communities in dealing with AIDS, explaining the need and opportunity for compassion.

A significant number of churches are taking positive steps to reach out to AIDS families. New policies were adopted, for instance, by the Broadway Baptist Church of Fort Worth in 1992, eight years after their failure to accept Matt in their Sunday school program. They discovered a need not just for an HIV-infection policy, but to strengthen their procedures to prevent the spread of infection from all kinds of communicable diseases.

In their written statement on the subject, they define an infectious disease as "any disease that spreads from one person to another person. This includes, but is not limited to, common childhood diseases such as chicken pox, measles, mumps, as well as more serious diseases such as hepatitis-B, HIV, and tuberculosis."

By acknowledging a responsibility to provide spiritual nurture to all children with every kind of disease, Broadway Baptist Church has succeeded in putting the

AIDS issue into perspective. Furthermore, they have done a thorough job of training their children's workers and parents concerning hygiene, use of rubber gloves, procedures for blood spills, and other common-sense procedures. If that program had existed in 1983, my family and perhaps many others would have been spared a great deal of grief and confusion.

Not everyone, of course, has an opportunity to give an AIDS awareness speech, or appear on television to discuss the topic. We may not teach a children's Sunday school class, or work with the children's-church ministry. But all of us have a responsibility to become informed about AIDS. Christians who want to obey the commands and follow the example of Jesus have a responsibility to reach out in loving compassion to those suffering with AIDS.

After all, the real question is not, What can the church do or What should the individual do? The crucial question for Christians is, What would Jesus do in the face of AIDS? For whatever Jesus would do is what his followers should do.

We can get a good idea of how Jesus would respond to AIDS victims in our day by watching how he dealt with leprosy victims in his. In Jesus' day, leprosy was a horrible, debilitating, incurable skin disease. The disease was considered so repugnant that nobody wanted to be near a person who had it. Most people ran away from a leper when they saw one. Healthy people feared they might contract the disease if they got too close. By law, when a leper walked down the street, he or she was required to warn everyone to stay away. To do so, lepers rang loud handbells and cried out, "Unclean! Unclean!" as they approached an uninfected person.

Jesus, however, was not afraid to touch a leper. He reached out to them in love, compassion, and healing.

In our day, AIDS has taken on many of the stigmas once associated with leprosy. AIDS victims are thought by many people to be unclean and untouchable. People are afraid to be near someone who has AIDS for fear that they will catch the disease. But there is little chance of that happening under normal circumstances. Our modern medical experts know more about AIDS than any other virus, and the evidence is overwhelming and reassuring that AIDS is not transmitted through casual contact.

What then can we do?

The first step in reaching out to AIDS victims with Christ's love and compassion is to become informed of the facts.

Human immunodeficiency virus, HIV, is the virus that causes AIDS. No cure currently exists for HIV. So, once a person is infected with HIV, he or she eventually will get sick. Unless a cure is found, those who get sick will die in a relatively short period of time, often within one year, and rarely more than ten years, after showing symptoms. The time between contracting the virus and showing symptoms varies greatly from person to person.

When a condition known as "immuno compromise" is reached, the person is said to have AIDS. At that point, the body's immune system has been broken down because of the disease, and can no longer protect itself against infections and other opportunistic diseases such as pneumonia and certain cancerlike diseases.

As such, the real danger of being around AIDS victims is not that you will catch something from them, but that you will spread germs to them that their body can no longer fight off. More often than not, however, the protest that "we do not want to endanger the person with the disease" is used as an excuse for ostracizing the victim of AIDS. The AIDS victim's doctor usually can tell when it is unsafe for the sufferer to have normal contact with the public.

One of the aspects that makes this disease so frightening to many people is its ability to avoid detection for so long. Any person infected with HIV, whether or not they have symptoms of AIDS, can infect another person. Nevertheless, AIDS cannot be transmitted by hugging someone with AIDS. Nor can you get the disease by shaking hands, being sneezed on, using the same toilet or water fountain, swimming in the same pool, or even eating from the same dishes as an AIDS-infected person.

Nor has there ever been a known case of AIDS being transmitted by a mosquito bite. The virus that causes AIDS is unable to survive for long outside the human body, making it extremely difficult to catch through normal casual contact with an infected person.

If AIDS is so difficult to catch, why are so many people contracting the disease?

AIDS is spread primarily in two ways: through sexual contact with an infected person, or through coming in contact with HIV-contaminated blood. Usually those who contract the disease because of contaminated blood are intravenous drug users who use needles and syringes used by other HIV-infected users.

It is *possible* (but extremely rare) to get AIDS from an infected doctor or dentist, and, as in the case of our family, it is possible to get HIV through a tainted blood transfusion. Mothers with HIV can pass the disease on to their children. About one out of four children born to HIV-positive mothers get the virus. Most people who get AIDS in America, however, do so through sexual contact.

The most explosive issue for the church or for individual Christians seeking to deal with AIDS patients caringly is homosexuality. Most sincere Christians have no qualms about helping people with diseases such as cancer or tuberculosis. Much of the unwillingness to confront the issue of AIDS relates to the disease's early homosexual connotations.

It is true that when AIDS first began to show up in America, many of its victims were homosexual men. Since the disease first flared into an inferno in the gay community, strong emotional and institutional forces interfered with the normal process of examination of the disease. For instance, the vested interests of the blood industry in America caused it to deny its culpability. For a variety of reasons, some valid and many not, people quickly came to regard AIDS as a homosexual disease. Comments such as "It's their problem. They should know better. They deserve it. Let them deal with it." became commonplace.

In truth, AIDS is not simply a homosexual disease. Granted, homosexuals, because of their sexual behavior are a high-risk group, but heterosexuals get AIDS, too. AIDS is not confined to one group or location. It has turned up in all fifty states in the United States and in every country of the world in which medical records are kept. In some countries, AIDS already has infected as many women as men, and more heterosexuals than homosexuals.

In the United States, AIDS is more prevalent among homosexuals. That creates a moral dilemma for Christian churches wanting to minister to AIDS victims.

Most Christians, although certainly not all, regard homosexual practice as wrong behavior.

The issue for the church, however, is the same one I faced when I discovered that my son Skip was homosexual. Because of my understanding of, and commitment to, God's principles as revealed in the Bible, I could not condone Skip's actions, but I continued to love him as my son, and as a person God created for a purpose.

Can we Christians overcome our prejudices and love past our theology to help meet the needs of dying people? I pray so. If we truly love the person, we can deal with his or her deviant behavior, whether it be dishonesty, thievery, drunkenness, promiscuity, drug addiction, or homosexuality. As we often say, but have a much more difficult time doing, the Christian is to hate the sin, but love the sinner.

Admittedly, such a biblically balanced position will not be universally applauded by the gay community. Nor will it be universally accepted by the "straight" community. But we will hear "Well done, good and faithful servant" from the One who counts, as we learn to love in the Spirit of Christ.

Those are the basic facts about AIDS, well documented in over ten years of research. Nevertheless, many people remain skeptical.

For example, recently I spoke at a meeting at the First Baptist Church of Plainview, Texas. At the pastor's request we had a session to discuss AIDS. Several doctors, nurses, and other caregivers were in the audience. After I told the story of my family's experience with AIDS, we had an open discussion.

An obviously educated woman stood to say, "We hear so much about this epidemic, but are you sure

they're telling us all the story? Are you personally satisfied that we are getting the facts on the contagion of
the disease and the ways it can be spread?"

I hear that question everywhere I speak on this subject. From Georgia to Washington, from Florida to
Colorado, the refrain is repeated, "Are you convinced
that we are being told the whole truth about AIDS?"

Unfortunately, an underlying distrust of government
and other public institutions in the nation works
against us at this point. Similarly, news media constantly are accused of giving slanted or inaccurate reports. Add to that skepticism the fear engendered by
the deadliness of the virus and the question is understandable.

Nevertheless, the answer is simple—YES! I am convinced that the truth is being presented. *The Harvard
Health Newsletter* (Vol. 19, No. 6, April, 1994) says it
well:

> A fear of contracting AIDS from casual contact
> compounds the stigma, although such transmis-
> sion is virtually impossible. Approximately 99.5%
> of infection occurs through sexual intercourse,
> shared needles, or transmission from mother to fe-
> tus. Although the virus could theoretically be
> spread through contact with saliva, urine, or feces,
> there is no evidence this has ever happened.

As we better understand how AIDS is spread, it becomes obvious that the best way to prevent infection is
to avoid the two main types of behavioral risks—sexual
immorality and intravenous drug usage.

The responsibility for teaching sexual values and discipline belongs to the family and the church. Unfortunately, both institutions have failed in these areas in

recent years. Furthermore, the cascade of media messages touting permissive behavior and the pressure of peers tends to make young people—or adults, for that matter—who exercise restraint in their sexual behavior seem odd and out of step.

Nevertheless, even here there is encouraging news, especially in regard to our nation's youth. Many church youth groups across the nation are creating counter-pressure groups that exalt biblical values of abstinence from sex until marriage, and sexual purity and fidelity within marriage. One such program used by Southern Baptist churches is "True Love Waits." In this program, young people sign commitments that they will remain sexually abstinent until marriage. Will some renege on their promise? Possibly, but many will keep that promise, and in doing so, significantly lower their risk of contracting AIDS.

Surveys are beginning to show that many teenagers are not sexually active. Actually, over half of American teenagers practice sexual restraint. That is good news from a biblical perspective, but it is also good news from the standpoint of AIDS prevention.

People who refuse biblically consistent and common-sense prevention methods are convinced that condoms can keep people from getting AIDS. The truth is condoms do count. And yes, they can help prevent AIDS transmission. But they must be used consistently and correctly to be effective.

And many Christian parents and leaders are concerned about the message free condom distribution conveys. They believe condom distribution promotes promiscuous behavior and weakens sexual discipline. Furthermore, some who advocate condom use often are offensive to Christians because of their attitudes toward biblical principles of sexual purity and sexual

self-control—proven methods of healthier relationships, as well as AIDS preventatives.

Promotion of condom use among people who already are infected with HIV can, however, lower the
risk of further contamination and spread of the disease.

How can a church begin a ministry to people with
AIDS and their families? For starters, talk about the
issue from the pulpit. If pastors are knowledgeable and
willing to speak on the subject, they can present the
information themselves. If not, host informed, compe-
tent, compassionate guest speakers—whom the pastor
can endorse—who will speak about AIDS and how the
church can respond to it.

Nancy Miller, a Christian, now works in AIDS education, after caring for her college-aged son, Stephen,
as he died of AIDS. Nancy arrived at the right conclusion when she wrote in *HIV/AIDS Ministry,* "If only
the congregation could say the 'A' word, then a
church-supported plan to minister to families caught in
the throes of HIV and AIDS could be instituted."

It is imperative that churches and synagogues adopt
and implement such plans. As the epidemic grows,
there are fewer people sitting in our sanctuaries who
have not been touched by AIDS. If AIDS has not hit
their immediate family, they have friends, colleagues,
neighbors, or extended family members who struggle
with the disease. Many faithful people in our congregations yearn to ask for prayer for AIDS-related needs in
their lives, or in the lives of friends. But they are afraid
to do so.

Regarding her family's reluctance to ask for prayer or
other support from the church, Nancy Miller wrote
that such a request "could only have been done had we
been assured of support and love. Understanding

would have been nice, too, but that may have asked for too much. How can one understand another's dilemma unless it has been experienced? We felt claustrophobic, afraid, and betrayed."

And that is a word from one of the faithful! Think of the myriad of people without the tenacity or spiritual commitment to hold on when they pick up signals of distrust and rejection from the church.

If churches are going to demonstrate compassion in the face of AIDS, they must recover their motivation for ministry. We will have to abandon what I call our "leave-it-to-the-Samaritan complex."

The best-known story Jesus told is the parable of the good Samaritan. The traveler on the Jericho road, set upon by thieves, wounded and bleeding beside the road, is a classic description of a person in desperate need of help.

A priest and a Levite, a sort of associate worship leader, passed by on the other side of the road, purposely ignoring the hurting man, so they could hurry on in their do-good missions for their religion. The surprise of the story is that it was a Samaritan who stopped, had compassion, took on the time-consuming task of rescue, and paid the bill for the traveler's treatment. Those actions alone are astounding in any culture, but to Jesus' original listeners, the good Samaritan's compassionate care was nothing short of earthshaking.

Those in ancient Israel never used the words *good* and *Samaritan* in the same sentence. Samaritans were despised by the Jewish religious elite. To a Jew, Samaritans were outsiders, a sleazy undependable lot, who had rejected a great deal of the Scripture and failed to live by what they had not rejected. Socially acceptable people did not even travel the road that went through Samaritan villages, preferring to cross the Jordan and circle around Samaria.

With this in mind, it seems outrageous that Jesus chose a Samaritan as the hero in his who-is-my-neighbor story. Jesus' main point, however, was not the Samaritan. It was showing that the religious institutions and their leaders were calloused and indifferent toward hurting human beings.

Has anything really changed? Is not this same sin still with us, taking a devious modern-day twist in regard to AIDS victims?

As Christians, we have been content to leave the care of those with AIDS to outsiders. AIDS victims and their friends and families have had to help each other while walking through its devastation. People in the fields of entertainment and the arts have been far ahead of the religious community in supporting AIDS victims. Even the medical and blood service organizations such as the Red Cross and the nation's blood banks had to be dragged into the struggle.

Who should have been the first to mount the parapets of this battle? The followers of the One who told that Samaritan story!

The motivation for Christians to get involved in an AIDS ministry is this: "For Christ's love compels us" (2 Cor. 5:14). In gratitude to Christ for loving us despite our flaws, we allow that kind of love to flow through us to others.

Jesus modeled for us how to treat people who exhibit unacceptable sexual behavior. The woman taken in the act of adultery (John 8:1–11) was brought to Jesus in hopes that he would endorse the vengeful crowd's desire to stone her to death. Significantly, Jesus bent down to write in the sand. It is as if he wanted to be eye-level with this battered woman despite her guilt. Looking up from where she is, he says, "If any one of you is without sin, let him be the first to throw a stone at her." The coldhearted religious hypocrites melted away under his searing gaze.

Christ's church was formed to be a place of fellowship and training, but also a place where flawed people could find help. Can we be captured afresh by Christ's example of love and forgiveness? Can that compassion be reignited as we focus on the hurting and dying of our day?

Part of the answer lies in the leadership of Christian churches. Public meetings that present the compassion of Christ and the complexity of the needs of people with AIDS can help churches recover our initiative for ministry, not only to AIDS victims, but to all hurting people.

In many cases, our spiritual leaders may need to become more knowledgeable about the disease. I confess, before my family was affected, I knew little about AIDS. I could rationalize my ignorance because the disease was so new at the time, but none of us can plead that excuse today. Information about AIDS is readily available, including how it can be prevented and how we can minister to those who have been affected by it. Every religious leader needs to know the facts about HIV and AIDS. For those seeking more information, the Centers for Disease Control in Atlanta can provide free materials.

The church also needs to comprehend how this disease rips apart social relationships. Normal support systems in our society often do not work for AIDS victims. Victims and their families often must deal with anger, blame, guilt, and shame. Exhaustion and fatigue characterize most AIDS victims and their families. It is easy for those affected to slip into self-pity and depression. Stress becomes a daily companion.

Ironically, churches are ideally equipped to respond to AIDS. When churches are at their best, there is acceptance; grace means "undeserved love." With adequate information about how AIDS spreads, caregivers can put aside fear and compassion can flow.

Practical support need not be complicated. One support group of friends prepared a weekly calendar for an AIDS family, listing the support group members' times of availability and ability to help. Each person noted specific segments of time and resources. For instance, one person volunteered himself and his auto Thursday afternoon from three o'clock to five o'clock. Another person offered thirty minutes on Tuesday to be available for the family if they needed anything.

Thanks to this simple calendar, the AIDS family could schedule help when they needed it—no searching frantically for assistance. This practical idea was a wonderful gift for a family that was house-bound while caring for a critically ill family member.

Simply being there for an AIDS victim and family members may be the most powerful ministry we have. We can visit AIDS patients in their homes, watch television with them, talk to them, and simply spend time with them. "Just being there" becomes increasingly helpful during the deteriorating stages of AIDS.

One of the saddest statements in the Bible came when Jesus encountered at the Pool of Siloam a man who was crippled from birth (John 5:1–15). When Jesus asked the man, "Do you want to get well?" he answered, "I have no one to help me into the pool when the water is stirred." There is no loneliness like that of people who have no one who cares.

It does not have to be that way. An AIDS family tells of a friend who called to say, "I'm bringing lunch today. I want to eat with you." The family members said that the food was helpful, but what meant most to them was the friend's presence at their table with them.

In his day, Jesus was accused of the ultimate social faux pas—he ate with outcasts and sinners. After all these centuries, we still have difficulty breaking the mind-set that we should associate only with "our kind of people." Yet if we are going to help raise the dead, we must go to the graveyards.

We also need to prepare for more people living longer with HIV-positive symptoms. Although every day of life is a blessing, and it is always possible that a cure may be found, a new challenge lies in how to handle prolonged anticipatory grief. Grief for HIV families is not brief and concentrated as it is with a tragic sudden death. It is long, often drawn out, and extremely painful.

Many AIDS sufferers, like Matt, now live with the disease for twelve years or more. Others who have tested positive for HIV but who have not yet developed full-blown AIDS are living with a death sentence over their heads. Someone who is HIV-positive faces every day wondering if this might be the day that AIDS symptoms begin to show up, and the disease begins to ravage his or her body.

Here again, Christians in general and Christian churches in particular, have a unique opportunity. Churches are on the front lines when it comes to dealing with grief. Love puts us there. The gospel deals with life here and hereafter. It is the source of hope and comfort to the soul facing death, and to those who face living through the dying of loved ones.

But AIDS takes so long, has so little hope, and carries so much fear and stigma that it is a unique kind of grief.

The stages through which an AIDS victim passes include a time of denial—"This can't be happening to me." Often, people in this stage do bizarre things trying to prove to themselves that the message of death is not true. Inexorably, numbness sets in. Lethargy often follows after being stunned by the awareness that death is indeed coming.

Usually sufferers and their families go through ill-defined but real emotional stages. Our family did. We went through times of weeping. The pain of facing that reality was so deep and the hurt so constant that we burst into tears at unexpected and inappropriate times.

Anger builds. The fact that life is not fair becomes an intolerable reality. Enraged by the events of our lives, we want to strike out. We often miss the target and hit at any target in close proximity. Those who love us often feel the brunt of our anger.

Depression ushers in a time of misery and fatigue. We begin to grieve for ourselves. We feel abandoned. No matter how many words to the contrary, we feel unloved. Somewhere in the process we try to bargain with God. He healed others. Surely he can turn the tide. What promise can I make? What deed can I do? What gritting-the-teeth kind of faith must I demonstrate?

We finally emerge with acceptance, ready for the struggle. We allow ourselves to think about the end that is coming. We settle our unfinished business with those around us. The hurt comes in spasms, as acceptance leads to anticipation.

* * *

For HIV and AIDS families and sufferers, all of these grieving processes come well before the actual dying experience. When the disease's progress slows long enough, these elements may show up, disappear, and then reappear. The grieving process is a nightmarish roller-coaster ride for many AIDS families.

Consequently, intense help from AIDS support groups is needed at the end. That period of time may be longer in the future than it has been in the past. We need to make our support-givers aware of that fact, and help them guard against burnout.

Another part of the church's compassionate response to AIDS involves the constant need to educate our constituency. Nothing can be more helpful to AIDS victims and families than for the truth to be known— that under normal circumstances, they are not a threat to anyone. This is especially true for children. Fortunately, many of the formerly widespread myths have been laid to rest, but not all of them. Moreover, misinformation about AIDS continues to find willing listeners. As such, education is an ongoing challenge for the church, and education does not happen accidentally. Once we know the truth about AIDS, we are responsible for educating others.

Compassionate people also must support and work for compassionate public policy. Public issues are complex. Differences of opinion are rife on solutions to civic problems. The tragedy comes when Christians do not care enough to form intelligent and informed opinions. Christian churches have a responsibility to urge their members to support research, to affirm the worth of persons regardless of their physical impairments, and to do everything possible to prevent this and other deadly diseases.

A final appeal to the church's compassion is to remember the AIDS victim's family after the victim is gone. A devout Christian woman in a southwestern state tried to help her pastor lead their congregation to understand that. What she got was silence.

She said, "My husband is a deacon in the church. I have sung in the choir for years. We are what they call 'pillars of the church.' Several months ago, we asked for prayer for our gay son who had AIDS. When our son died at his home in California, my husband informed the pastor. Our pastor's only comment was to ask whether the funeral would be in California or here. We still attend the same church and see the pastor and people every Sunday, and often throughout each week. No one has asked how we are doing or how we are dealing with our grief. All we have gotten is silence."

Grief does not end at the grave. Neither should caring people abandon families as they exit the cemetery. Healing some wounds takes time. It certainly takes loving presence and sharing of hope.

AIDS is not going to go away any time soon. The prognosis is not good. Many doctors and scientists despair of ever finding a cure for the disease. Certainly, no cure is coming in the near future. Consequently, we need to learn to deal with the disease, and the sooner the better.

As Christians responding to AIDS, or any other crisis, we are to demonstrate Christ's love. Love in action is the only kind of love there is.

TWENTY-FOUR

THE BURDEN
LIFTED

"YOUNG MAN, YOU won't do your finest preaching until you have been through Gethsemane." The tall, thin, freckled old man peered over his rimless glasses, and reared back in his squeaking chair as he delivered the declaration.

I sat uncomfortably on the edge of my chair. My dad sat nearby. Lean, muscular, and over six-feet tall himself, he and Pastor Earl Anderson towered over me. I felt comforted by Dad's presence. He had been ordained as a pastor in this church by this man. The small office in which we sat was tucked away at the rear of the Munger Place Baptist Church in east Dallas. The year was 1945, and I was seventeen years old. Ten years before, I had been baptized a few feet away from where we sat.

Now I was a youth evangelist and Dad and I had come to talk to Pastor Anderson about my ordination to the gospel ministry. Pastor Anderson agreed to lead the questioning in the ordination service. I wanted to ask him the questions I'd be facing, but didn't have the nerve to do so. This was one of those exams you could not cram for, and spent your life preparing to take.

Pastor Anderson chose this occasion to give his advice, words of wisdom he considered key to genuine gospel ministry. His words were like a slap in the face. I could not understand why this elderly pastor would stifle my youthful enthusiasm. I didn't appreciate his comment, and I didn't understand it. I was too polite to argue, so I simply tucked his words away for future reference. His comment didn't make much sense to me at the time. Besides, Gethsemane seemed a long way off.

Of course, as a pastoral candidate, I knew what Gethsemane represented in the life of Christ. Gethsemane was the garden outside Jerusalem's walls, where, on the night before Jesus was crucified, he went to pray and to wrestle with the inevitability of his death. The meaning of Gethsemane is derived from the process of making wine. Gethsemane is the place where the grapes are pressed down, to squeeze out the juice for the wine. It was an intensely stressful place for Jesus. Stress can reach no higher degree than it did that night when Jesus cried, "Father, if it be possible, let this cup pass from me: nevertheless not as I will, but as thou wilt" (Matt. 26:39 KJV).

To Christians, the Garden of Gethsemane is the universal symbol for agony and suffering. When Pastor Anderson told me that I wouldn't do my best preach-

ing until I had experienced Gethsemane, he was saying
that effective preaching is born in the crucible of pain
and suffering.

It has been more than fifty years since Pastor Anderson gave me that profound admonition. The old
preacher was right. And I believe I am just beginning
to understand what he meant.

The mid-1980s through the mid-1990s was the decade of Gethsemane for my family and me. Four family
members—a daughter-in-law, a son, and two grandsons—were diagnosed with the AIDS virus. My best
friend died of a stroke, which I attribute to the stress
AIDS placed upon him. We dealt with the AIDS virus
on two levels. On a medical level, we found out the
facts about the disease and fought it. On a spiritual
level, we journeyed into our individual hearts to seek
God's wisdom. For a long time, like thousands of other
families who struggle with this disease, we attempted
to care for one another in secret. The burden of that
secret became increasingly heavy. Now, thankfully, the
secret is known and the burden has been lifted.

I once watched a diamond cutter strike his crucial blow
on an uncut diamond. He had studied the gem for
some time. The moment he struck the large stone
sharply with a mallet and cutting tool, the gem flew
apart. But what remained was incredibly beautiful.
Some of the fragments themselves would also be valu-
able, but the diamond would never be the same again.
As I watched the diamond cutter pick up the remaining
stone, and hold it so the light could shine through it, I
suddenly realized that the diamond's greatest gift—
that of reflecting light—would never have been evident
without the shattering blow.

My family is similar to that diamond. A smashing

blow has been struck. The fragments of that painful experience lie all around us. None of us can ever be the same.

Nevertheless, God is shaping diamonds out of what would be rubble in the hands of anyone but the Master Craftsman. My prayer is that the diamonds that come from our experience of being shattered will be cut and shaped so we can best reflect his light.

Despite our differences, my family members share an obsession with God and an obsession with life. Our obsession with God is expressed differently by each individual, but it is nonetheless real. And because of our shared experiences with grief, suffering, and death, each of us recognizes anew that the gift of life is too precious to be taken for granted.

Wanda and I are grateful that all of our sons—Mike, Skip, and Scott—have found healing and help in different ways. Twelve-step programs have proven helpful in their healing processes. The acceptance and mutual support found in such programs acknowledges God's help without demanding uniform definitions. That has been important for my sons.

But that does not mean that we are out of the valley yet.

Our oldest son, Mike, still has the deep-seated problem of inner fragmentation. Long after he became free of substance abuse, he still is lonely and lacking in social ease. His schizophrenia is under control, but it has left its marks on him. Anger and panic often trouble him.

In his journey, Mike wrote poetry, took courses in community college, read portions of philosophy, and talked about God. Many of Mike's and my conversations through the years have been late-night sessions at Jim's Coffee Shop in San Antonio. Mike is one of those whom religious institutions often allow to fall through the cracks. It takes too much time and energy to meet the complex needs of people with his disorder.

Yet he takes God seriously. He deals with the implications of the Sermon on the Mount and the sayings of Jesus. He is honest and conscientious about meeting his responsibilities. His feels that churches don't want "people like me." He cares, but doesn't have the social skills for communicating that care.

I have had to learn to let him be. For far too long, I tried to rush to his rescue every time he had a problem, and I usually did more damage than good in the process. Today, we love each other, stay in touch with each other, and still go to Jim's to talk about, and to, God.

For Skip, the damage has been done by judgmentalism and rejection. There is an honest lament, as well as anger, in his description of the damage done by organized Christianity to people with whom he walks. Consequently, he has distanced himself from the organized church. Nevertheless, he is deeply devoted to Bible study and prayer, and has an open dialogue with God.

In his prayers, Skip often sounds like a psalmist or an Old Testament prophet. I am intrigued by the way Skip boldly approaches the Father, and asks, "What are you doing to me? Why would you lead me to do this project in my business and then leave me hanging until the last minute before you come through? I know you're going to do it. You always do. But why do you have me stretched out like this? Do you enjoy watching my anxiety build before you act?"

God is real to him, and the joys and sorrows of their conversations often are close to my own experience.

Skip knows he is dying of AIDS. He is not yet heavily medicated, although he does take the natural nutrients that briefly helped Matt. Skip optimistically told me the other day, "I think that I may have about three years to live, the way these nutrients are working."

Skip spends most of his time working in his art gallery and picture frame business. But he always finds time to encourage people in the homosexual community who are dying with AIDS. Within that community, Skip helps men and women face death and prepare for it. He already has prepared for his own death. He says, "I'm at peace about that. I'm right with God. I love Jesus. I'm not afraid to die. I would rather go on living, but I'm not afraid to die. My life is going to be shorter than most people's, but a lot of people's lives are shorter than mine. I'm going to try to make my life meaningful, and make it peaceful."

Skip has lived through so many deaths in our family in recent years, he has been able to put his own death into perspective, and he's not afraid. He feels a sense of calm and peace about it. Skip sometimes quips, "There is a lot more apprehension about living than there is about dying."

Despite Skip's upbeat, positive attitude, Wanda and I know we must be prepared to walk again through the valley of the shadow of death.

As I write these words, Scott's disillusionment with the church is so deep that he has turned to Eastern religions. He joins me in an obsession with God, but his terminology and concepts differ from mine. Yet we frequently find common ground in our conversations about God.

One day he said, "Dad, I know what you are thinking. You think I am going to come around to Jesus again someday."

I simply smiled and replied, "All I ask is that you

keep on reading the Bible. Let the Gospel of John be one of the things you read."

He replied, "I will, if you will read the *Tao Te Ching* [the basic book of Taoism]."

I said, "It's a deal."

In carrying the burden of the secret, Scott carried the heaviest load of us all. He took the brunt of the church's rejection of his family because of AIDS. He was forced to scramble to make financial ends meet, and to keep some sort of insurance coverage for his sick family members. As the only healthy person in his home, he carried most of the household chores, as well as the responsibility to care for Lydia and Matt. He lost his wife and baby to AIDS. He poured twelve years of energy into being the best father he could be to Matt. No one could have given more of himself.

Sadly, the hurt continued for Scott even as Matt's life slowly slipped away. The short time Matt was expected to live stretched into month after month, adding stress to Scott and Mary's marriage. In a traumatic time of emotional pain, Mary and Scott decided to separate and divorce. The wounds of well-intentioned dreams gone awry are some of the saddest by-products of a devastating disease like AIDS.

Wanda and I continue to pray for our sons. That is not all we can do for them, but it is the best we can do for them. Meanwhile, the Spirit of God is at work drawing all men unto himself.

For me personally, my family's experiences have been instruments God has used to break the safe little chambers I would have constructed for my life. Emotional illnesses cause millions of people to live their lives emotionally crippled and halting. I would never have had to grapple with that truth if Wanda had not known the agonies of depression as she dealt with her bipolar personality. Her courage and candor in dealing with it is inspiring.

I never would have been aware of the frightening realities of a world filled with terror if Mike had not been fractured and wounded by paranoid schizophrenia. To see him functioning normally today with the help of medication is a miracle I couldn't have understood.

I would have sought a seat in the balcony of humanity to observe the phenomena of homosexuality if Skip had not forced the issue by declaring himself gay. His obsession with God challenges me to deal candidly with truth and reality.

The easy answers I had about pain and suffering and God's plan for it were crushed by the HIV virus that cursed half of my family. I would have missed so much if my grandson Matt had not come to demonstrate to me how to live day-to-day with a deadly disease. In many ways, Matt taught me not only how to live, but also how to die.

I never would have fully grasped the greatest truth of all—that God is greater and larger than religion—if my son Scott had not been so damaged by church institutions.

My piece of that old paradise from my boyhood church was forever lost. I have had to pick among the broken pieces to find what cannot be shaken. And I have found diamonds in the rubble.

No, the Garden of Gethsemane has not been pleasant. But while there, just as God sent his ministering angels to Jesus, God has sent ministering angels to encourage me along the way.

I rejoice that over the years of the journey ministering spirits have come to me in the stress points of my life. I have needed more than an impression or a vision or a dream. Therefore God has clothed his messengers in flesh and blood and intersected my life with theirs at crucial points.

The angels I encountered didn't have wings and auras of light. They are people that God has given me, people through whom God is communicating to me, and they come almost eerily timed to the exact moment of my need. The encouraging messages come from people unexpectedly, and speak to me in ways that nurture and strengthen me.

That kind of mystery causes me to live life with joy, because I know that whatever difficult Gethsemane experience is coming, it is also going to be accompanied by the strength of an angel. The messenger of God is going to remind me of the mystery of God's presence in my everyday life.

At one of the lowest points in our ordeal with AIDS, I was deeply touched by a man from Wisconsin who sent me a cassette tape of a sermon I had preached back in 1974. He was in tune with us and understood what we were going through. Along with the tape came a note, saying, "As I was hearing this, I made a copy for my wife, and I thought you might want one, too."

I put the tape in the tape deck and turned it on. Sure enough, I heard myself speaking on the subject of encouragement. My message was based on a scriptural passage written by the obscure Old Testament prophet, Habakkuk:

Though the fig tree does not bud and there are no grapes on the vines, though the olive crop fails and

the fields produce no food, though there are no
sheep in the pen and no cattle in the stalls, yet I
will rejoice in the LORD, I will be joyful in God my
Savior. The Sovereign LORD is my strength; he
makes my feet like the feet of a deer, he enables
me to go on the heights. (Hab. 3:17–19)

As I listened to the tape, I was astounded. The message spoke to me about my attitudes and my relationship with God seventeen years later. I listened as I told
what God had said to me seventeen years earlier.
Amazingly, it was true right now, and I needed to hear
it! I needed to be reminded of the truthfulness of that
passage of Scripture.

It was a moving, mysterious affirmation and correction that God gave me. The man who sent that tape
became a messenger of God to me. After all, that's
what angel means—"a messenger from God."

God does not leave you alone in your Gethsemane.
He is always there for you in your need. Your only
responsibility is to trust him. Before the ministering
spirits can come, though, you must be able to say,
"Not my will, Lord, but Thy will be done."

We live in a pain-filled world; everybody hurts to
some degree. Your pain can increase your capacity to
be sensitive to someone else's pain—if you allow it to
do so. Pain can cauterize you, creating scar tissue that
makes you less sensitive. Or it can open you. But regardless of what you go through, God will meet you
on the level of your understanding, and at the depth of
your need.

I don't pretend to understand why my family has had
to carry the burden of the secret. All I can say is that I
am thankful that burden has been lifted.

Someday I will understand it all, when I see Jesus face-to-face in heaven. There will be no secrets there.

Lydia was right. We don't know much about heaven, but we know it will be a great adventure. Actually, it will be the greatest adventure of all. The good news is that we do not journey where no one has traveled before. One has returned to say, "Do not be afraid."

In heaven there will be no limitations of time, no more weariness and fatigue, no aging; all death and disease will be gone forever. We will see our loved ones who have gone on before us. I am going to see my dad, and Bryan . . . and Luke . . . and Lydia . . . and Matt. We will have unbroken fellowship throughout eternity. Most of all, we will see Jesus, the One who makes the Peaceful Place possible.

And the mystery is no more.